SO-AEZ-748

CELESTIAL HARMONY

CELESTIAL HARMONY

A GUIDE TO HOROSCOPE INTERPRETATION

MARTIN SCHULMAN

SAMUEL WEISER, INC.
York Beach, Maine

First published in 1980 by
Samuel Weiser, Inc.
P.O. Box 612
York Beach, Maine 03910

Reprinted 1982

Copyright © Martin Schulman 1980

ISBN 0-87728-495-4

Typesetting and layout by
Positive Type
Millerton, N.Y. 12546

Printed in the U.S.A. by
Noble Offset Printers, Inc.
New York, N.Y. 10003

Contents

...To you, whose enduring search for truth carves the path of future understanding...

...To you, whose questions open the doors of inspiration and light the windows of hope...

...To my dearest little Princess, Penny Sue, whose crystal stream of love glistens through the waters of my soul...

Author's Note

Nature's seasons are an integral part of man's consciousness. Metaphorically, they symbolize the rhythm of change through the natural process of evolution. While it is understood that on a physical level, the seasons vary in different parts of the world, it should be clear that the true meaning of seasonal changes is found in consciousness. Thus, the four seasons symbolize distinct modes of thought and being which all individuals regardless of locality experience as a natural part of the ebb and flow of their lives.

One might question how difficult it might be for an individual living in the Sahara desert to imagine the experience of snow. Yet, it has snowed in the Sahara. In Northern climates it might also be difficult to envision the experience of warmth. Yet, there are times that are appreciably warmer than others. Even in places where seasonal changes are subtle, man still has the opportunity to know the difference between the four basic modes of consciousness that God has provided. Thus, when we think of astrology in terms of nature expressing herself through seasons, we are approaching the source of man's connection with that which makes him grow.

The concept of equal seasonal changes is easily visible in the northern hemisphere. But, the experience in consciousness of seasons changing is far more universal. Thus, if one can view astrology through this foundation, one can grow more in touch with the true source of all experience.

For everything there is an appointed time,
 even a time for every affair under the heavens;
a time for birth and a time to die;
 a time to plant and time to uproot what was
 planted;
a time to kill and a time to heal;
 a time to break down and a time to build;
a time to weep and a time to laugh;
 a time to wail and a time to skip about;
a time to throw stones away and a time to bring stones
together;
a time to embrace and a time to keep away from
embracing;
a time to seek
 and a time to give up as lost;
a time to keep
 and a time to throw away;
a time to rip apart
 and a time to sew together;
a time to keep quiet
 and a time to speak;
a time to love
 and a time to hate;
a time for war
 and a time for peace.

Ecclesiastes 3: (1-8)

The reader is asked to understand the astrological derivation from seasons, then, as the language through which celestial change is imparted to man's consciousness.

Martin Schulman

Introduction

As the oldest and most complex form of understanding known to man, astrology holds within it the keys to finding out all there is to know in the universe. Naturally, one could never attain the ability to understand so much. But, on a practical level, even a small part of this knowledge has the potential of being the greatest tool for solving our problems.

Astrology pierces deeply into the very core of man's essence, stripping away the sham of his superficial outer layers and bringing to light the quality of his true being. But, what is an astrologer? Is he a mathematician? Is he a researcher? Is he a social scientist? Is he a counselor? Is he a philosopher? Is he an analyst? Is he versed in different religions? Is he a teacher? He is all of these, but, he is, first, last and always, a humanitarian. He should be an individual who cares about what happens to his fellow man. And, perhaps most important, he is always a student, forever learning.

The astrologer deals with individuals on all levels and of all ages. He must understand human·behavior, human cycles, human relationships, the business interests of his clients, their cultural and religious differences and how a myriad of environmental influences affect their destinies. Thus, the astrologer is a Master student all his life.

He studies people; their ways, habits, their successes and their failures. He observes their actions and reactions. He understands human emotions on the very deepest of levels. And, he is an excellent student of nature. He watches the seasons change, and he becomes aware of cyclic activity. He sees the leaves on a tree and learns how they are dependent on the branches from which they grow. He notices that no branch looks exactly like any other. Yet, it is impossible for him to decide if one branch is better or worse than another. From this he realizes the individuality and the equality of people.

If he is truly aware, he can see the connection between man and nature on many levels. For what man seeks his entire life, the trees know. The seasons know. The rain and the snow both know. But man does not know. And, it is the purpose, job, and function of the astrologer to be able to tell man in words that he can understand, that he is truly able to achieve the same harmony with natural law that he sees all around him, if he will only look.

Thus, astrology is a very different kind of language, and the astrologer is an interpreter of nature's music to man's ears. The entire purpose of this study is to put man in harmony with nature, so that he can feel as sturdy as the mountains, as gentle as the first snowfall in winter, as musical as the leaves that feel the wind blowing across their surface, and as happy as a child's smile revealed by knowing that God's blessing is everywhere, all the time, and that in all of nature's glory, man is exhalted the most.

The Horoscope is a Symbol

The astrologer uses a circular wheel and divides that circle into segments in order to translate zodiacal symbols into meaningful language. The chart is not a map of an individual's life any more than a photograph of a tree is a map for the future growth of the tree. Each is a symbolic representation of reality. Why is it important to understand this? Astrology students often become immersed in the symbols they study and lose the essence of the science. They begin to talk as if people were signs and symbols, guinea pigs for future research or marks on sheets of paper. Human beings are often converted into triangles, squares and crosses.

The good astrologer remembers that the picture of the tree is not the tree. And, should he look at the picture incorrectly, turn it upside down, accidently scratch it, or fail to notice how many branches and leaves there are, he knows that this has no effect on the real tree itself. The natural quality of reality, its essence, flavor, smell, color, and beauty is in no way influenced by an photograph one would take of it. Unless the student understands that the horoscope is a "symbol" of a person's reality, but not the reality itself, he can easily make the mistake of forming habit patterns which tend to dehumanize his fellow man, reducing the fullness of that very special human quality that changes and grows and blossoms in its season.

The horoscope acts as an intermediary between the astrologer who knows how to translate its symbols into language, and the very human individual who needs to order that language into concepts which make sense to him. What comes out of the horoscope can show a person how to build shelves in their mind, shelves which will be filled eventually with their own encyclopedia of nature's understanding and the Divine plan in which their role plays such an important part.

For example, consider an individual who takes a test in school. Seeing an "A" on the piece of paper, he reacts emotionally to the paper, never fully realizing that the paper is not what he is reacting to. He is in fact reacting to the results of his efforts which is, after all, the reality in this instance. The paper is very much like the photograph of the tree. The teacher who graded the paper could be considered analogous to the photographer. Thus, the student cannot thank either the teacher or the paper for the grade he received, for both are outside of the reality of his personal circumstance.

If the grade is poor, than all it means is that the individual can do better if he so chooses. The same is true of a horoscope. One is not "cursed" with a bad chart. The astrologer should know that life can express in different ways without those ways being necessarily better or worse than other ways. This is the beauty in the world. These are the colors of difference and change that make life so vividly fascinating!

God does not create a "bad" or "evil" person. A rosebush can become overgrown with love's neglect. That does not mean that the rosebush was born for a bad or evil purpose. And, with care and pruning, it is possible for that rosebush to *re-form* and bloom in full beauty. This is the basic point of astrology. Man is a part of nature. He blossoms with love and care and little by little is able to realize the potential that his horoscope symbolizes. Large trees with thick layers of bark (that may be compared to individuals we think of as being stubborn) seem to grow appreciably better when they sense the presence of love. If a tree can be that sensitive with all its power and strength, imagine how much easier it is for man to respond to the same harmonic music of nature's way.

The horoscope helps us to understand the way an individual can best be tuned to all that nature has to offer him. The chart may show negative tendencies, faults, problems and difficulties—in essence, all the things that make man the beautifully imperfect creation that he is. That is fine. Suppose every mountain, river and stream were perfect in exactly the same way? Where would the beauty of nature be? The beauty of man is not in his perfection, but in his *imperfection*, for through his realization of imperfection he has reason and purpose to grow more beautiful. And, it is through astrology that he can find his way.

The astrologer, then, is an observer of natural law. Through what he sees, he comes to understand the harmonic qualities of man in relation to his environment and to himself. But, this is only part of the picture. This is the intuitive natural understanding that one can develop over the years. Certainly, it is a talent. Indeed it is a fine art through which one can see the subtle shadings and blendings of colors, sounds, sensations, and forces that make up the world. And, depending upon one's ability to be sensitive to what is happening around him at all times, makes the extent of understanding that one astrologer has quite different from another.

Still, this is only an incomplete picture, for astrology is also a definite science. Specific rules and guidelines have been established through many years of empirical research by thousands of dedicated individuals. The scientific formulas in astrology have been, still are and will always be tested for their validity. Through this process, the science grows more valid, more accurate, and more able to pinpoint its statements in very practical ways. Astrology is a science of truth. But, from a scientific standpoint of view, what is truth? Philosophers believe that truth is that which gets right to the core of something and that truth has a "smell" to it that one can feel through one's very essence. They don't know this, but everything within them leads them to believe it. Thus, from a philosophical point of view, truth is really—a belief. If one were to see the logical extension of this, then truth for any individual becomes whatever he chooses to believe! On a certain level of thought, there is validity to this. But, astrology, although it would be helpful to mankind if it were founded through this type of thinking, could never really grow to its true potential. This is where the scientific approach to astrology becomes extrememly imporant. To the scientist, "truth" is that which is provable until it is disproved. In this sense, if a statement can be proved accurate ninety-seven percent of the time, as opposed to a contrary statement which can be proved accurate only forty percent of the time, a scientist will accept the first statement as a "truth." Even the law of gravity under certain scientific test conditions does not work one hundred percent of the time. But, for the practicality of the very real world we live in, it is accepted as a "truth." And, so it should be; for truth should be based upon the blend between that which is "absolute" as an ideal, and that which is able to come the closest to it through our limited ability to perceive the totality of the universe in which we live.

Thus, astrology is both an art and a science. To look at it either way without considering the other is to miss the point entirely. From nature, man observes phenomena that makes him question. The answers he comes up with must be scientifically tested in order for him to know that they are valid. When he knows that they are, it creates a belief in him that gives him the faith to search for more. Thus, he goes back to nature again and observes, and through this process, man slowly comes in contact with his spiritual self and the true reality of what exists. Astrology is a tool, a language, a vehicle for man to unfold his greater being to see himself as an integral part of the natural world he lives in.

The Nature of Coincidence

*B*efore the student can attempt to understand the horoscope, he must confront the question of *coincidence*. Is there such a thing as coincidence or is there not? When this question can be answered it is possible to begin to understand the cosmic laws which play such an important role in man's existence.

According to the Thorndike Barnhart Dictionary, coincidence is "the chance occurrence of two things at such a time as to seem remarkable," or an "act or fact of occupying the same time or place." Another way to define coincidence is to say that it is the observance of things which seem so unlikely that we are able to ascribe their causes to "chance occurrence." Thus, the question of coincidence is really the question of whether or not "chance occurence" occurs without rhyme or reason.

To confront this question, one must first realize that the universe is ordered according to specific cosmic laws. Thousands of years ago, man did not have much knowledge of these laws. As a result, whatever he could not understand would be ascribed either to "coincidence" or "superstitious beliefs." As science developed ways of researching and measuring the things that man could not understand, those individuals who think so different from us that it is superstition gave way to knowledge, and coincidence gave way to a sense of awe at how remarkably ordered the world really is. Today we have a greater sense of cosmic law. The gap between what we know and what really *is* still leaves room for people to believe in "coincidence" and "superstition." But, the more this gap closes, through research and scientific discoveries (which are observably provable) the less meaning the words "coincidence" and "superstition" actually have.

Consider a common occurrence with which most people are familiar. An individual moves away from a place where he was living, says goodbye to his friends and does not see them for years. Then one day, he meets an old friend on the street, and says "Isn't it a coincidence? I was just thinking about you last week!" The first thing to consider is how many people does this happen to? And why do they always follow it up with the thought or statement that "It's a small world?" Let us examine the situation in more detail and see if the world "coincidence" is really applicable to such a situation.

Let's look at the middle experience first, because it actually happened first. The statement, "I was just thinking about you last week," says a lot more than it appears to say on the surface. One individual will think about another because his thoughts are moving in the same direction as his friend's on a certain level of consciousness. One thinks about another because of what the other *stands for*. It is man's way of reaffirming that he is not alone in the constant questions and answers that keep going through his mind. Thus, like attracts like. It is not remarkable that they should meet, for in the same way that a supermarket displays different brands and varieties of the same product together on a shelf, the world of thought arranges itself so that similar thoughts attract each other. This is provable. We tend to reject from our lives and our consciousness clear different wavelengths exist and we are attracted to individuals who seem to be "on our wavelength."

Thus, the statement "I was just thinking about you last week," shows the actual time when the two individuals met in thought, for their consciousnesses were both moving toward the same place. The thought that "It's a small world," is certainly true in consciousness, because when it comes to thought there are no obstacles such as space distances or gaps in time.

Would it be considered a coincidence if two individuals independently decided to go shopping? No. They both had the same need. If they met at the supermarket, it is only because the store serves the common need in both. Thus, is it remarkable that they should meet? Not at all. In this light the "chance occurrence" of their meeting is not as statistically remote as to even approach the "awe" that usually accompanies what one calls "coincidence."

Consider another example in terms of whether or not "coincidence" exists. An individual goes out on the street and meets a friend of a particular zodiac sign. Later that day another friend calls who is the same sign. In the evening, still another individual of the same sign comes into the person's life. On the surface, this seems to fit what we call "coincidence." If this phenomena is observed a little more realistically, it appears to be something quite different altogether. Our lives are structured from our unconscious which is constantly calling out through telepathic messages to the conscious mind. When an individual's unconscious is going through an insecure period in life, it will bring a lot of Taureans into the person's environment. When an individual is ready to make fresh starts, his unconscious magnetizes itself to attract Arians so that he can learn how to make these starts from the Mars energy. Is it really a coincidence that we notice certain signs in our lives for a while? Then, almost as miraculously as they were there, they disappear and people of other signs appear. Actually, this is not a coincidence at all. It is just a very human way of learning the lessons that help us grow.

The more one studies the universe and the laws that rule it, the more one begins to doubt that there really is such a thing as coincidence. Of course, we cannot be sure of this because we do not know everything about the universe. As our knowledge increases and our consciousness expands it becomes increasingly reaffirmed that if we ever did know everything in the universe, we would realize that nothing is coincidental!

If one believes that there is "coincidence," then one is cutting himself off from the unfailing source of supply that is part of the natural ecological chain that brings everything to fulfillment. Astrology (as science, art, philosophy, or perhaps as a future religion) does not subscribe to any belief in the word "coincidence." It says that there are truly remarkable things in the universe, and as a result of this there are awe-inspiring occurrences in our lives. For some of these things, we are aware of the reasons. For others, we become aware of the reasons years later. For still others we may never know the reasons. But there is a reason for everything. Einstein, one of the greatest geniuses in history said, "God does not throw dice with the universe." If circumstances and events occurred without rhyme or reason life would be flat, toneless and purposeless, never prompting man to ask the question he is always asking: "Why?" Astrology encourages this question and says, "Let us try to find out."

Where Do I Begin?

Since there are many good textbooks available about methods of chart construction, and since charts can be ordered through competent astrological computer services, the subject of how to erect the natal horoscope will not be discussed here. Chart construction is never the student's real problem. Reading a chart, or being able to understand the symbolic implications in a chart is the real difficulty. Thus, the student is usually confronted with the questions, "Now that I have the chart, what do I do with it? What does it all mean? Where do I begin?"

In a complete interpretation of a horoscope the factors to be considered are quite numerous. One must understand the elements, the modes, the planetary placements and their relationships with each other, the full meaning of the signs, houses, cusps, decanates, the Moon's nodes, certain Arabian parts, retrograde planets, chart patterns, cycles, transits and progressions. These astrological symbols indicate specific feelings, experiences, circumstances, and states of becoming and being that individuals go through. Even the experienced astrologer is confronted with the problem of synthesizing all of these factors into the clearest description of "truth" that is valid and usable to the client!

Thus, the question, "Where do I begin?" becomes extremely important in terms of helping the individual to develop a method of reading the horoscope. It should be a well-ordered system that will progress from the beginning of a person's life to the period of growth in which the person is now involved.

Astrology always works from the vague to the specific. Life is that way. An individual may feel vaguely confused when he begins to realize that he has problems. By the time the problems are almost solved, he is specifically clear about what he is doing in terms of dealing with them. If horoscope interpretation starts by trying to be specific then one is apt to zero in on some facets of the individual's life while entirely missing others. The astrologer needs a method which allows him initially to grasp the full essence of the person. He should both sense and know the information that he is assimilating without drawing any conclusions about it. He should then be able to take this information and refine it through a process of discrimination, carefully sorting how bits and pieces of information are related to each other. Finally, he must focus in on this information so that he can transform it into the wisdom necessary to help solve the client's problem. At this point, when he has reached the finest focus possible, and senses that whatever understanding the client is capable of at the current time has been achieved, he must move out of the specific and back to a vaguely detached and impersonal attitude in terms of what the client (of his own free will) ultimately chooses to do with all he has learned. Thus, chart interpretation begins with an impersonal distant view of the forest. Then it moves specifically through each tree, often touching sensitive spots in what appears to be very personal ways. But, to put the picture in focus we need to include a view of the entire forest as each tree in it understands its function. The interpretation of any horoscope is a process of moving into an individual's space, getting close enough to fill the gaps, patching the wounds of karmic sorrow, and then moving out of the individual's space, without carrying the client's life experience as a part of your own.

It is the goal of every astrologer to be as accurate as possible while leaving to the client a small "coefficient of inaccuracy" that Dane Rudhyar calls the "coefficient of free-will". But, before any degree of accuracy can be achieved, the astrologer must know how to prepare for a reading. There have been many astrologers who have read horoscopes for people without realizing the importance of the atmosphere surrounding the encounter.

Preparation for Reading Horoscopes

If a chart interpretation is to be beneficial to the client, then the astrologer must know how to achieve a neutral state of mind within himself before he begins. If he fails to do this, it is very easy for him to unconsciously read things into the chart that are not really there, but are his own tensions and conflicts which get projected from the back of his mind during the interpretation. It is one thing to look for something in a chart. It is quite another to impersonally approach the chart as a new experience, without preconceived notions about what the chart might say. If one is constantly looking for something in the horoscope, one will always find it. By looking for something specific, it is not only possible but highly likely that the astrologer can give too much weight or priority to what may be a projection of his own unconscious.

In order to minimize this effect, it is helpful if one knows how to spend a few quiet moments in meditation before approaching the chart. This frees the mind from all of the accumulated tensions it has been holding, and allows the astrologer to approach the horoscope with a much more objective and unbiased point of view. If one is not familiar with meditation, then a few quiet moments alone in contemplation will help to free the mind of unnecessary blocks that would hamper good understanding and communication. I have found that by looking at a plant, a bush, or a cloud for a few minutes helps put the mind in tune with nature and frees it from preconceptions that might enter into a reading.

The next thing to consider is that there will always be a vibration created when people discuss their problems. To many, this vibration is unseen, but it does create tension and emotional strain which stays in the air for quite a while after the reading. Many astrologers work from their homes, and inadvertantly expose their families to these vibrations. One can walk into a room where a reading has just been completed and feel the tension in the air! When one considers that some astrologers give as many as five to ten readings a day, several days a week, one begins to understand why so many astrologers live alone. This does not have to be, however, if one is conscious of the kind of energies that readings involve. You can learn how to handle them. If an individual makes the effort to physically clean the room, dust the furniture, open the window, etc. after each reading, then such tensions are minimized to a point that they do not have to have such a strong effect on the private life of the astrologer. If it is possible to do chart interpretations in an office, away from home, so much the better? A man's home is truly his castle. Far from being a cliche, it is the fortress that protects him and allows him to rejuvenate from all the tensions of the outside world. If he systematically allows the problems of others to invade his "castle," then he can weaken himself to the point where he is really not as helpful to others as he would like to be. Thus, whenever an astrologer can strengthen himself, elevate his consciousness, and remain objective, he is doing himself, his clients, and the future of astrology itself a great service.

The next thing to understand is that man is capable of worrying without realizing he is worrying. The initial contact between astrologer and client occurs on higher planes of consciousness, the moment the client decides to call the astrologer for help with his problem. The appointment for the reading might be weeks in advance, but the client has already unconsciously telepathed the nature of his problem to the astrologer. Thus, the astrologer experiences an unconscious link to the energies of the chart he will read, long before he even draws up the chart. For this reason, it is important to learn how to remain sensitive enough to understand people's problems, while at the same time realizing that they are "unreal." This takes much training and discipline and does not happen overnight. There are many ways that one can reach such an understanding. The would-be astrologer can learn how to achieve such a disciplined consciousness from metaphysical schools, spiritual books, and enlightened teachers.

Consider, if you will, the individual who comes to the astrologer in a state of anxiety about his finances. The person may be so emotionally overwrought that his palms are sweaty. The experienced astrologer understands the reality of the problem rather than its illusion. He understands that the client needs counselling about his response to his financial problem as well as the problem itself. It is reality that the successful astrologer deals with. It is the myriad of illusions created by emotions that bring him his clients. A good helpful astrologer is able to break people's illusions, so that they can free themselves from fighting what is not, and begin to deal with what is. Even the projection of one's problems to another is an illusion, but this is one of the most difficult illusions to master. Through practice, and discipline, however, the astrologer slowly learns by his mistakes, and eventually develops the very stern discipline necessary to do this kind of work.

The question then, "Where do I begin?" has nothing to do with the horoscope itself, for that comes later. The answer every student of astrology must always remember is, "I begin with myself!"

Looking at the Forest

*O*ne day, years beofre I had written my first book, I was browsing through a New York bookshop. Little did I know the important role that the thousands of volumes and ideas around me would play in my life. I was a student then, eagerly seeking new ways of understanding how to interpret a horoscope. As I browsed through the shelves, I happened to overhear a young man telling another, "Do you know how I interpret a chart? I look at the design it makes and then I close my eyes and see how that design makes me feel." I laughed to myself, thinking that this was the most ridiculous thing I have ever heard. A few short weeks later, the conversation came back to me and out of curiosity, I tried it. Much to my astonishment I noticed that different designs did make me feel differently. Some made me feel angry, some smooth, some threatened, some elated, some depressed, in fact, a full gamut of things I had never imagined. What was even more amazing was that these "so obviously ludicrous designs" correlated completely with the individual's life pattern they represented. If we give some thought to this, we can easily realize that anger is pointed, while love is round, elation is vertical, struggle is horizontal, etc. Studies of handwriting analysis show the same thing. Thus, there is a message in chart shapes and patterns if we are keen enough to objectively understand it. The question this raises, however, is: What is the reliability of first impressions?

First impressions always occur with the initial contact one experiences in meeting new people, new situations, and dealing with new circumstances. An impression has a vague quality. We trust it, but often not enough to interest us to investigate the feeling to determine if the impression is accurate. When students take tests in school, they are cautioned not to change their answers because the answer that comes to their mind first is usually the correct one. Notice here that the word "usually" leaves enough doubt as to give the student the freedom to mistrust his first impression.

When we meet new people we form instantaneous impressions. We receive whatever the individual is projecting. But, our receptivity is often limited because our perception is influenced by past experience. We say, "He reminds me of...," and then sink into viewing whatever unconscious memory patterns we can surface.

First impressions are powerfully valid if our perception is objectively clear. Even when we are somewhat biased, a good deal of what we initially perceive eventually turns out to be accurate. When we first look at a forest from a distance, we are struck by a first impression. The rather vague shape and feel of the Gestalt whole is assimilated by the mind. Then we walk into the forest to see all the intergral parts that make up the whole. When we leave the forest, the memory we take with us is really our "first impression," somewhat refined, clarified, supported, and perhaps corrected here and there by a few of the details that we studied closely.

As an art and a science, astrology combines "first impressions" with scientific data. Thus, when looking at a horoscope one first sees the shape and form that the chart makes. This occurs before we even discriminate one planetary symbol from another, much like we see the forest before knowing if the trees are maple, oak, birch, or how many of each there are and where they are placed in relation to each other.

The ability to assimilate the horoscope in a first impression is a fine art which can be developed through observation. Through the ages, astrologers have observed nature and natural processes. If one ignores the natural first impression received from a chart, one might miss seeing the forest altogether; and in studying the details within the chart may in fact mistake one or two trees for the entire forest.

The art of observing the Gestalt whole of the horoscope is the very essence of simplicity. The science of understanding the detailed facts which either support or negate such observation is extremely complex. Both compliment each other enabling the interpretation of a horoscope to be accurate and complete. Without seeing the whole, it is possible to interpret a chart accurately but through the wrong slant. By seeing the whole, but not studying the parts, it is possible to give an interpretation that is complete, but too vague to be useful. When intuition combines with mathematical science chart interpretation becomes quite a remarkable experience.

There are four charts on the following pages. Try to cast aside previous knowledge as you look at them. Do not study the charts in detail, but simply glance at each one for a few seconds. As soon as the shape and design seems less important to you than the specific planetary placements, degrees, etc. you have already gone past your "first impression" and are starting to be attracted to the colors of each individual tree in the forest. At this point, put the chart down, and record on paper your first impression. After you have done this with each chart, check your impressions with the actual facts (see page 20) of who these four individuals are. If you find that your first impressions were extremely accurate, start to trust them more. It means you are keenly intuitive, and able to grasp the true essence of something right away. Wherever there is the slightest element of doubt, the science of astrology should eventually dispel or affirm what you perceive. If you find that your first impressions were not accurate at all, you need to develop clear-mindedness so that your perceptions are not colored by personal distortions.

CHART #1: GEORGES PIERRE SEURAT (Painter)

The evenly balanced distribution of planets is an indication of harmonic perspective. There is proportion and rhythm to the design formed within the chart. Rather than seeing an overly heavy concentration in any area, we find a more gentle but wider scope of experience.

CHART #2: FRANZ KAFKA (Author)

Here we find a heavy concentration of planets together, indicating a rather one-sided view of life, but at the same time a powerful ability to focus energies towards expression. Intense gathering of different planetary energies indicates the dynamic qualities of the individual and hints at there being something rather special to be manifested.

CHART #3: HANS CHRISTIAN ANDERSON (Storyteller)

Here we see planets in all the quadrants, indicating breadth of experience. But, at the same time, there is a subtle see-saw quality that hints at a less than serious attitude towards life.

CHART #4: SIGMUND FREUD (Founder of Psychoanalysis)

A powerful intense concentration of planets on one side of the chart shows focusing ability along with intent to dynamically express some form of meaning. The singleton in the opposite hemisphere completes the bucket pattern which is often found in charts of individuals who have something important to carry.

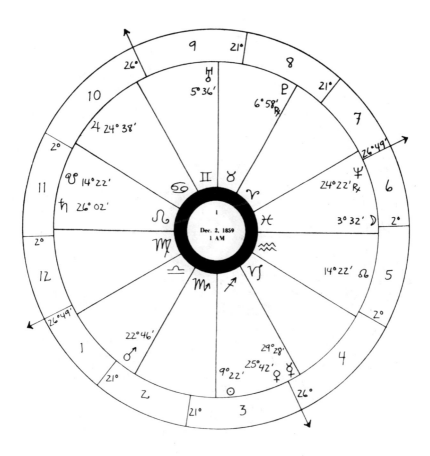

Birth data obtained from "The Circle Book of Charts" by Stephen Erlewine. Circle Books, Ann Arbor, Michigan, 1972, p. 54.

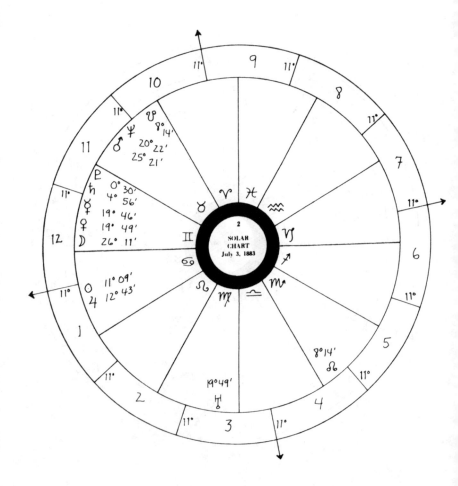

When looking at a solar chart, the emphasis on understanding should be placed on the signs and their natural placement in the zodiac rather than on specific houses which can be misleading.

Birth data obtained from "The Circle Book of Charts" by Stephen Erlewine. Circle Books, Ann Arbor, Michigan, 1972, p. 80.

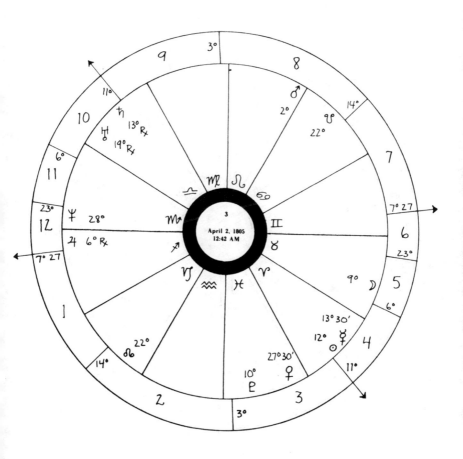

Birth data obtained from "The Circle Book of Charts" by Stephen Erlewine. Circle Books, Ann Arbor, Michigan, 1972, p. 28.

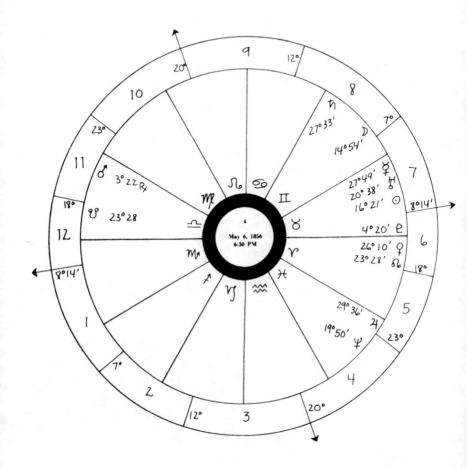

Birth data obtained from "The Circle Book of Charts" by Stephen Erlewine. Circle books, Ann Arbor, Michigan, 1972, p. 50.

Now that you've looked at the "forest" there is something else to consider. No matter what your first impression of a forest might be, you will discover when you walk through it that some trees are hidden behind others. Initially you may not have realized they were there! Try not to lock into first impressions too strongly, for their value lies in helping us to sense something, to experience something, but not to physically or mentally possess it. If you do, you will not allow yourself to see the trees that are hidden because something in you will feel that it already knows. Thus, put your first impression in the back of your mind as you begin to study the rest of the chart.

Be aware that *Every tree in the forest must fit into the forest, but not every tree in the forest is like the forest!* If you remember this, you will be able to maintain a balanced perspective as you interpret the entire horoscope.

Interpreting the Elements

A strology represents the universe in terms of the four basic elements. Traditionally, Fire, Earth, Air, and Water are the elements upon which all ancient philosophy is founded. It has been traditional to study them in this exact order. There is, however, a much more interesting approach which adds a great deal of insight into the way in which these elements become a part of horoscope interpretation.

All birth (the beginnings of things) is from Water. It is the universal solvent. When the element Earth is added, then plant life is possible. Both Water and Earth are unconscious elements. The water flows, but it is not conscious of flowing. The plant grows, and although it is sensitive to many things, it is not conscious of itself. When the element of Fire is added, then animal life is possible. Here we find our first glimpse of consciousness. An animal is capable of preventing himself from running into a tree because he is conscious of the tree and the effect it would cause him to experience. He does not desire the experience, therefore he walks around the tree instead of running into it. Thus, he is conscious. Still he is bestial because his instincts and behavior patterns lack a growing mentality. This ability to make use of a growing mentality is indicative of the Air element which symbolizes thought and is reserved for man. Thus, the Water signs (Cancer, Scorpio and Pisces) and the Earth signs (Taurus, Virgo and Capricorn) all have an unconscious quality to them. They have instinctual knowledge and intuition. They are highly sensitive to their environment. They don't think as much as they feel nature's forces. This does not mean that individuals born in these signs are incapable of thinking. It means that whatever thinking they do is based on impulses they receive from their unconscious sensory awareness of what is happening in the world around them. The Fire signs (Aries, Leo and Sagittarius) and the Air signs (Gemini, Libra and Aquarius) all have a conscious quality to them. Rather than receiving unconscious stimuli from their environment, they tend to be less dependent on what is happening around them. They are less rooted, easily moveable and as a result, more concerned with what they are making happen! From this, one might draw the conclusion that the Fire and Air signs have a definite advantage over the Earth and Water signs. And, if one looks at this further, inasmuch as reality or its appearance seems to constantly impress itself on the Earth and Water signs while the Fire and Air signs are able to impress their appearance on reality, the advantage seems even more pronounced. The fact is that the Earth and Water signs are more sensitive. Most great works of poetry, music, art, and the aesthetics come from the receptive abilities of the Earth and Water signs. The Fire and Air signs provide the spark and stimulation of ideas upon which culture is built. Thus, the differences which seem to give the conscious elements advantages over the unconscious ones really cannot be compared. The unconscious elements have enormous depth that the conscious elements do not have. Still, they cannot be compared for it would be much like saying "compare a plant with a dog." They are different things, performing different functions. Each has its place. And, most important—*each element sees reality in a different way.*

Water Signs

It is important to understand the qualities of the elements. When we think of *Water*, we think of wetness, fluidity, movement, reflection, washing, cleansing, purifying, baptism, and we sense droplets, rivers, streams and oceans. One of the principles of physics is that *"water always seeks its own level."* Thus, if you have a U-shaped tube and pour water into either side of it, it will rise in the other side to equal the height of the original side. This is important when we consider that Water signs are emotional signs. It is a clue to understanding that emotion keeps seeking balance. Individuals who are highly emotional rarely make much sense. Whatever emotion there is must equal its own level by another emotion. This explains why people who are emotionally happy tend to attract sorrowful people into their lives. People who are emotionally strong tend to attract people who are emotionally weak. Thus, the waters of emotion balance themself regardless of what form they take. It is the way of nature.

The emotional water signs live by what they feel. Cancer, Scorpio and Pisces are highly intuitive and psychic signs. They sense rejection, loneliness, fear, sorrow, anguish and love much deeper than other signs in the zodiac. The water element gives one a rich life in the world of feelings. The individual responds to changes in the weather in much the same way as a plant will turn towards the direction of the Sun. Instinctively, he will respond to changes in the unconscious moods of those around him.

One of the properties of Water is that of individual reflection. Depending upon whether the Water is calm or rough the reflection will be clear or distorted. The three Water signs are reflectors of unconscious emotion. As such, there is a great deal of "illusion" involved with the Water element. It is not so much reality, as the changing appearance of reality which concerns this individual. The only thing that appears "real" to a water sign, is *how something feels.*

Earth Signs

The Earth signs see reality in a different way. Taurus, Virgo and Capricorn concern themselves with the physical-material, form, matter. They are sensitive to the solid structure of *things.* In this sense, they are not as aware of "what is becoming" in the way that the water signs are, as they are aware of "what is." The securing, holding, firming up, the assurance of stability, are all qualities of the Earth element. There is a functional quality to the Earth element insofar as it relates to that which is useful, showing little interest in that which is not. Things are made for use. They have a purpose and must be able to serve that purpose, otherwise they are not useful. If we think of the qualities of Earth, we think of dirt, sand, rocks, trees, and everything that springs forth naturally from the Earth. These are the materials used for building structures. It is interesting to note that while the water element, because of its unconscious emotional sensitivity, wants to feel all that nature offers, the earth element wants to build structure in order to insulate and filter out much of nature's forces. It does this by building from nature's own fiber. There is a steady quality here not found in any of the other elements.

Earth supports and sustains. It is the soil of life, containing within it the substance from which all springs forth. The three Earth signs have the quality of containing their substance so that they can put it to the best use. They are concerned with preserving whatever is important to them. Quantity is an outpouring process, but quality is an indwelling process. The earth signs are concerned with the quality of things. What is the quality of an idea, a person, an object? From the quality one can ascertain the substance and then understand what is worthwhile and what is not.

Thus, what is "real" to an Earth Sign is the *quality that something contains.*

Firesigns

The Fire signs see reality in still another way. Aries, Leo, and Sagittarius seek to expend creative energy. When we think of the element Fire, we think of heat, light, sparks, flames, brightness, brilliance, and the Sun itself. Creation does not exist without fire. An automobile starts with a tiny spark, so does the inception of an idea. The heat of sexuality is necessary for the sex drive to impel one to action. In all areas, the Fire element impels action. It calls attention to that which would otherwise go unnoticed. Through this attention all else starts to function.

The Fire signs have a quality of excitement about them. Bursting with energy and vitality, they light up the dormant ideas in others so that thought can become action. Here, it is not so much quality, but the quantity of quality that is important. In other words, the concern is with the outpouring of the dormant indwelling quality. Potential energy is meaningless to a fire sign. The kinetic or active energizing of things becomes the focus of attention. Many variables are available for possible connections, but nothing happens until these connections are made! Connections occur through the magnetic attraction between things, people, and ideas that separately symbolize one thing but through connection can be something more than the sum of each put together. Fire signs, therefore, are centers of attraction to stimulate, to bring together for creation all that which has the possibility of vivid intense beauty, but cannot become it without the Fire element. One may have all the ingredients of a gourmet meal, but nothing happens until the stove is turned on! Thus, "reality" to a Fire sign is always concerned with *making something become* or the *act of creating!*

Air Signs

The Air signs symbolize the fourth way of looking at reality. Gemini, Libra and Aquarius concern themselves with thought. The idea of something is more vivid to them than the thing itself. When we think of the quality of Air, we think of lightness, non-containment, that which is intangible, breeziness, mobility, loftiness, invisibility, and usually a general sense of softness. This last quality is often where people make their biggest error in understanding the nature of the Air signs. Air is by far the most powerful element because it can go through any crack. Fire, Earth and Water are much more easily containable than Air, for what can contain thought? It is man's highest reality, for as he thinks so he is!

The Air Signs seek knowledge, with the gaining of wisdom as their ultimate goal. They identify with what they know and experience insecurity with what they do not know. They are constantly in the process of exchanging ideas with others so that a dissemination of knowledge is possible throughout the world. Air is flighty and independent, but that is the only way it can freely carry thought. Air rises above Fire, is not bound by Earth, nor does it lose itself in Water. Man's mentality as it is symbolized by Air is above sea, plant and animal life as represented in the other elements. The ability to *think* is man's greatest gift! Through this gift, he can question the order of the universe and increase his understanding of it. But, a gift is not a gift unless it is used. Man must learn how to think, for only when he does is he able to rise above his lower nature. Thought inevitably leads to higher forms of thought and symbolizes that very special human quality of seeking. This quality creates interest in what life is all about. Thus the Air signs, as thinkers, seekers, concern themselves in the reality of relating. How do ideas relate to each other? How do people relate to each other? How do different realities relate to each other? The true "reality" of the Air signs is *What is the nature of reality?*

• • •

An individual must stay in touch with his Element in order to feel comfortable. If one were to take a statistical survey of the number of individuals who go south for a winter vacation, the results might show that a large number of them are Leos whose attraction to the Fire element of the Sun draws them closer to the equator where they can experience their element in all its fullness. Pisceans are usually attracted to the sea, for it enriches their entire being. Each zodiac sign finds its own methods of staying in touch with its' natural element. When an individual is in touch with his element a great deal of the time, he is able to keep himself in high spirits, feel greater vitality, and function better towards whatever his purpose is. When an individual is far-removed from his element he feels out-of-touch, non-functional, and cannot keep his energy level at an optimum. It is interesting to note that the likelihood of a wish or prayer coming true is greatly increased if it is made at a bonfire at the seashore. Why is this so? It is the one place where the four elements, Water, Earth, Fire, and Air come to meet.

Interpreting the Elements in the Horoscope

The most important thing an astrologer can do is to help an individual to get in tune with himself. We have our first impression-looking at the forest. As one gets closer to it, the nature of the trees becomes visible. Some forests have twenty percent oak, forty percent maple, thirty percent birch, and ten percent pine. Other forests have quite a different balance. This is exactly what happens in the horoscope. By counting up the elements of the signs in which the planets appear, one can know if he is dealing with a pine forest, or a maple forest, or whatever blend the elements show. The dominant element always shows how the individual can best become in tune with himself. Sometimes, there is an element missing. This indicates a vibration that the individual tends to experience through others. An individual with no Fire planets may have great capabilities, but needs others who are in touch with the Fire element to initiate him to connect those abilities and put them into action.

Whatever the rest of the chart may say, the trees will remain within the forest, and the types or kinds of trees they are must be the particular tonal colors that make up the forest. The elements act as a tuning device through which the rest of the forest gains its texture. Here is where the impartiality of the astrologer is extremely important. On a personal level he may not like or be familiar with the kinds of element combination that a particular chart represents, but he must interpret the chart through those elements if he is to be of help to the individual.

The Seasons and Modes

*I*n the northern hemisphere the year is divided into four unique qualities we call seasons. In each three month season we experience a different part of the complete cycle. The astrological year begins in spring when the fresh vitality of nature's beauty emerges from under its winter blanket of snow. The streams melt. The ice turns to water, and the earth softens to give birth to new life. The air has a warm vibrant quality and the Sun breathes promise into the fresh seeds, nurtured over the winter, that now begin to show the first patches of greenery that will soon blossom.

The zodiac signs, Aries, Taurus, and Gemini fill the spring season with the promise of the coming year. The youthful quality of these three signs is very much like the early buds on the trees and the gentle new-born blades of grass, vibrant and vivid in their color, but not yet reaching the maturity of their divine potential.

As spring gives way to summer, nature's buds come to full bloom. Color is everywhere. Activity is heightened. The days are longer and more sunlight shines on nature's creation. Everywhere there is a ripening quality as leaves, buds, and plants give birth to flowers, blossoms, and food.

The rhythm of natural fulfillment is on display.

The zodiac signs, Cancer, Leo and Virgo fill the summer season with the enriched tones of perfect light as they bring to fruition the earlier promise of spring. There is a clean scent to the air as nature's most gentle fragrance enhances the pure essence of her natural beauty. The crops grow full and assure man of his sustenance for the year.

As summer gives way to fall, the joy of the harvest is everywhere. What was promised in spring and looked at in summer may now be picked and eaten. Everywhere it is a time of reaping what has been sown earlier. Nature is giving so that man can receive his cosmic legacy.

The zodiac signs, Libra, Scorpio and Sagittarius fill the autumn season with the changing colors of natural beauty as nature poignantly surrenders her bounty. Here the quality of ripeness reigns supreme. Man eats of the fruit, not the flower. From the literal cornucopia of nature's abundance, he receives the bestowal of God's promise.

As the fall gives way to the winter, the trees grow bare. Their bark stiffens and they turn their life inward. Streams and lakes freeze over to protect the life below. The gentle snow forms a blanket of inner warmth to shield the roots and seeds for another season. It is a time when nature conserves herself by concealing her preparation for the new cycle.

The zodiac signs, Capricorn, Aquarius and Pisces fill the winter season with the mature understanding of nature's divine purpose. Here the subtle mystical quality of that which is not seen acts to preserve the future. Nature sacrifices showing all of her beauty until the time is right in the new season.

Thus, we see the quality of the twelve zodiac signs acting as part of nature's quality. Each has a specific reason and purpose. And, should nature be missing any one of her twelve children the completeness of her magnificent plan would not be possible.

The Modes

Astrology sees three qualities in nature that symbolize the trinity of her intention. We call these Cardinal, Fixed and Mutable modes of the behavior of natural law. The Cardinal bird is an American songbird with bright red feathers. The Cardinal flower is a bright red flower. Both attract initial attention to themselves. In astrology, a Cardinal sign begins a new season. Aries is the initiator of spring. Cancer is the initiator of summer. Libra is the initiator of fall. Capricorn is the initiator of winter. Thus, through the Cardinal signs we see the beginnings of nature's four phases. They have the quality of *interest* which serves to energize each phase so that it can progress to it's natural outcome.

Individuals who have their Sun in a Cardinal sign are always expressing the initiatory quality of nature. In whatever they do, they are forging ahead to find new pathways, create trails with no footsteps ahead of them, and explore all that is yet to be discovered. If a person does not have a Cardinal sun sign, but does have other planets in Cardinal signs, then those planets will take on this same quality as they forge their way into the future, starting seasons in consciousness for others to build on. The primitive quality in the Cardinal signs matures as the year progresses. Aries shows the youthful pioneering spirit through whose enthusiasm the year begins. Cancer is somewhat less primitive, but as it gives birth to the summer season it nevertheless represents beginnings. The difference is that now a sense of care, nourishment and warmth is added. In Libra, where we see the beginning of the fall harvest, a more matured sense of delicacy, balance, and harmony of mind is manifested through a sense of fairness and decency. When the final season begins in Capricorn, we see the bigness of ageless wisdom expressing itself through man's concern for preserving qualities which are more meaningful than his personal self. Thus, the concept of making beginnings can be manifested in four different ways. Man can begin to plant a seed (Aries). Or, he can begin to fertilize the growing plant (Cancer). Or, he can begin to harvest its fruit (Libra). Or he can begin to prepare the soil for future use (Capricorn).

The word Fixed symbolizes that which is firm, steady and ordered in its ability to sustain a stationary quality. A Fixed Star moves only two degrees every hundred years. Thus, its position is dependable. Trees grow new branches every year, but their roots are firmly fixed in the ground. Thus, where a tree was before, we can expect it to be in the future. Such is the reliable, sustaining quality of the Fixed signs. The four Fixed signs are always the second or middle sign of each season. Each one in turn sustains and supports the quality of the season through its reliability and dependability. Taurus is the Fixed sign in spring. Leo is the Fixed sign in summer. Scorpio is the Fixed sign in fall, and Aquarius, the Fixed sign in winter. Although each season begins in a Cardinal sign, it reaches the fullness that gives it its identifiable quality through the stable characteristics of the Fixed sign. The Earth sign Taurus identifies spring as much attention is focused on the mellowing of the earth for planting. The Fire sign Leo identifies summer as its warmth and brillance brings nature to her bloom. The Water sign Scorpio identifies fall as nature gives the outward appearance of hiding away her beauty and ending her cycle. The Air sign Aquarius identifies winter through nature's impersonal silence as she prepares herself for the unexpected qualities of the future.

Individuals who have their Sun in a Fixed sign are always expressing a "digging in" quality that symbolizes nature's sense of involvement. They seek solidity, dependable reference points, and try to manifest a dynamic quality that will leave a deep impression in whatever they do. Through this there is a sense of permanance that comes from all that a Fixed sign represents. If a person does not have a Fixed Sun sign, but has planets in Fixed signs, then those planets will display the same qualities of "central-ness", strength, and dependability, as they manifest the involution and purpose of nature's power. As the year progresses, the Fixed signs fulfill their purpose through an upward evolutionary spiral. In Taurus, we see the primal solidity of Earth as it prepares to accept the seeds of spring planting. In Leo, we find a more sustantiated sense of brilliance that shines through a powerful dynamic quality, but still does not move from its fixed center. Scorpio symbolized a more mature quality that understands the importance of endings. Still, the fixed nature of the sign never fluctuates from its purpose of destroying that which is no longer useful. Finally, in Aquarius the impersonal idea for mankind's evolution is manifested. But, because it is a Fixed sign, the ways in which the ideas for change are expressed are in and of themselves rooted to a higher sense of permanance that never truly changes.

Thus, the Fixed signs represent different means of permanence through which mankind develops a sense of purpose and fulfillment. all the meaning found in life's reliability comes from the Fixed signs.

The word Mutable means change. Once each season has been initiated and preserved it must gracefully surrender itself to the following season. The impact of each season as it begins in Cardinal signs and the sustaining power of each season as it seeks endurance through the Fixed signs becomes muted and mutated as it surrenders its power for the following season. The Mutable signs then, always show the decline of one season along with the anticipation of the next. Here we find nature manifesting her intention of impending change. Gemini symbolizes the ending of spring as it changes into summer. Virgo symbolizes the ending of summer as it changes into fall. Sagittarius symbolizes the ending of fall as it changes into winter, and Pisces symbolizes the ending of winter as the melting snow changes into the sparkling streams of early spring. There is duality in these Mutable signs as both the giving up of one season and the reaching for another are occurring at the same time.

Individuals who have their Sun in a Mutable sign are always expressing the yin and yang quality that is inherent in all forms of change. They can see fault in the old, and doubt in the new as the past withering away before their eyes forces them to need the unknown quality that is the future. Thus, a sense of uncertainty pervades all thought and action that emanates from these signs. If an individual does not have a Mutable Sun sign, but has planets in Mutable signs then these planets will express the changeable, non-committal, turning over of nature in her mode of surrender. In the same way as the Cardinal and Fixed signs, the Mutable signs also show a spectrum of evolutionary progress as the year unfolds. In Gemini we find a rather shallow gentle cleavage between spring and summer as man through his lower mind begins to understand the concept of duality. Virgo in a somewhat more sophisticated manner attempts to understand a sense of order amidst a world of separating particles. In Sagittarius, we find a more mature attitude towards change and movement as man's higher mind tries to comprehend the "all" of things through a wide spectrum. Finally, in Pisces there is the intuitive understanding of no form at all as the entire year surrenders itself to its creator.

Thus, we see how the twelve months of the year fall into four cooperative seasons which follow each other according to nature's order, and how each season is initiated, preserved and changed through the Cardinal, Fixed and Mutable modes.

The Masculine-Feminine Quality

*T*he Masculine-Feminine quality is present everywhere in nature. While this is generally thought of as sexual differences, it has an even greater meaning. Masculine is a quality of giving, outpouring, overtness, that which is above the earth, consciously creating changes, extroverted, expressing the positive nature of light, while Feminine is a quality of receiving, indwelling, that which is below the earth, unconsciously experiencing changes, introverted, and playing the receptive role of darkness receiving the light.

The Masculine and Feminine qualities represent the yin and yang of creation. The Yang or Masculine principle symbolizes movement and activity sweeping across the Yin or Feminine principle which passively receives it. Neither quality is better or worse than the other. Instead, they compliment each other much like day and night, figure and ground. Day is the masculine positive quality through which all creation shines, but it is during the night that the silent process of photosynthesis takes place. Thus nature often grows in darkness while it receives sustenance and displays itself in daylight. Man heals spiritually and physically when he is sleeping. He does not grow or heal as much when he is awake. Instead, he becomes aware through light of what he has achieved in darkness. If light may be equated to joy and darkness to suffering, it is the suffering that enables man to know what joy is. A figure cannot exist without a background. A background has no meaning without a figure. Thus, figure and ground or that which approaches (Masculine) and that which recedes (Feminine) need each other in order to exist. Musical compositions contain loud (Masculine) passages which must be offset by soft (Feminine) passages to obtain a balanced contract. Odd numbers express the masculine quality. Even numbers contain the feminine quality. In the very atoms that make up matter, we find positive and negative ions complimenting each other to produce the whole. A coin has two sides (heads and tails). The tendency is usually to prefer "heads" (or the masculine quality) but without both, the coin could not exist.

The direction *north* is a positive or Masculine quality, while *south* is considered a negative or Feminine quality. In the physical body, negative energy is released through one's feet, while positive energy is expressed through the head. The point is, that although there is a very important difference between the Masculine and Feminine quality on many levels at the same time, neither supercedes the other in the functioning of God's most ordered universe.

One may think that the Masculine quality represents greater physical strength than the Feminine. This is not the case at all. Looking directly at nature we learn that a glacier is three times as deep (the feminine quality than it is high (the masculine quality). The roots of a plant while staying hidden beneath the earth (the feminine quality) can often survive weather conditions that the rest of the plant above the earth (the masculine quality) cannot. Individuals experience an inner and an outer life. Their inner life, their consciousness, is a feminine quality. Their outer life, the masculine expression of this quality is often less fulfilled. At the same time, one should not draw the conclusion that the Feminine quality is necessarily the stronger of the two.

It is not! There is very little that can resist the masculine force of the wind as it sweeps across the earth creating changes in her essentially feminine nature. On levels of thought, it is a Masculine quality to express an idea (the light shining on the earth) while it is a Feminine quality to be receptive to the idea (as the receiver of the light). Thus, in many ways we are able to see the Masculine and Feminine qualities acting and receiving action as the most simple expression of natural law.

The Fire signs (Aries, Leo, and Sagittarius) and the Air signs (Gemini, Libra, and Aquarius) all possess the masculine quality. The Earth signs (Taurus, Virgo, and Capricorn) and the Water signs (Cancer, Scorpio and Pisces) all contain the Feminine quality. For this reason, the Fire and Air signs are called the Conscious Signs, expressing themselves above the earth, while the Earth and Water signs are called the Unconscious Signs, receiving and observing nature's creation. Fire and Air sign individuals tend to make the world happen, while earth and Water sign individuals observe and seek understanding of what is happening to them. Thus, through the masculine-feminine qualities, we see two distinctly different perceptions of reality. Both are correct. Both necessary.

Since the odd numbers carry the masculine quality, the odd-numbered signs are considered to be masculine in character. The even numbered signs are the feminine signs. As one moves through the zodiac they follow each other in succession; always a masculine sign leading to a feminine sign.

Like the alternating currents of life, the seasons lead into each other. The zodiacal year beginning with spring starts with a masculine sign. Summer which receives the thrust of spring's surge begins with a feminine sign. Fall acts to harvest the fulfillment of summer and begins with a masculine sign. Winter is the result of fall's harvest and begins with a passive feminine sign, as the earth rests in preparation for its new cycle.

WINTER   –   +   FALL

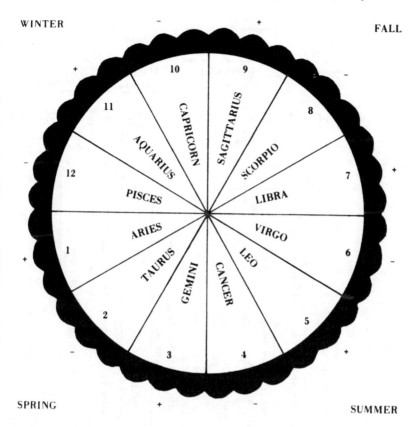

SPRING   +   –   SUMMER

    To clearly understand the masculine and feminine quality of each sign it is important to study the quality in the context of its *season*. An enthusiastic student may assume that because Aries and Aquarius are both masculine signs that the masculine quality in them is identical. In Aries, the masculine quality acts to begin the year. It asserts itself boldly. In Aquarius, the masculine quality acts to liberate the year from its self-history. Thus, the masculine quality of Aries asserts itself to project into all that will be, while the masculine quality of Aquarius asserts itself to project out of all that was. As a result, Aries becomes a sign that leads to involvement while Aquarius acts to achieve non-involvement.

	SPRING			SUMMER			FALL			WINTER		
Purpose	Promise Planting			Fulfillment Growing			Harvest Reaping			Conserving Hiding		
Signs	♈	♉	♊	♋	♌	♍	♎	♏	♐	♑	♒	♓
Quality	+	−	+	−	+	−	+	−	+	−	+	−
FUNCTION	Activity to initiate involvement	Indwelling container (womb) receiving creation	Actively divides that which has been fertilized	Protective concealment for birth, (embryonic sack, the sap in the tree)	The Outpouring potential, bloom on display	Observing the perfect creation, the fruit	Nature acts to balance her receiving by giving back	The taking out from the earth	Activity for the reaping of Abundance	Indwelling return to original form	Change to achieve disinvolvement	Surrender of form for dissolution

Notice how each Sign leads to the next and how the Masculine (positive) and Feminine (negative) qualities are colored by the season in which they function.

Consider the feminine quality of Taurus, whose passive nature symbolizes the earth receiving the seeds of spring. Pisces also has a feminine quality, but because it is the last sign of the year, its purpose is to acquiese and surrender the winter by dissolving itself into spring. The differences between these two feminine signs can be understood when one realizes that Taurus is a part of the spring (whose purpose is to build form in solid soil so that the season can achieve its fulfillment), and Pisces symbolizes the energy necessary to allow the year to dissolve. The understanding of the masculine-feminine qualities of all the signs can be achieved in similar manner. The quality of the sign is always acting to fulfill the purpose of the season.

The Inner and the Outer Planets

*A*strology and astronomy both observe a difference between the planets close to the Sun and those farther away. All of the planets up to Mars (Mercury, Venus, Earth, Mars) are called the *Inner Planets* while the planets beyond Mars (Jupiter, Saturn, Uranus, Neptune, Pluto) are called the *Outer Planets.* The asteroid belt between Mars and Jupiter (which we believe is pieces of an unformed planet) clearly separates the division between these two sets of planets.

Since the solar system is as much a part of nature as that which we perceive here on earth, the differences in characteristics between the Inner and Outer is important to observe.

The first distinguishing feature is the difference in movement and rotation. A day on Mercury is approximately equal to six hours on Earth. In contrast, a day on Saturn (one of the outer planets) is approximately equal to twenty eight years. The time difference varies greatly between inner and outer planets, and this difference becomes extremely noticeable in the way we feel its influence on Earth.

The second important difference is in the relative size of the Inner and Outer Planets in comparison to each other.

The approximate difference between Venus (an inner planet) and Jupiter (an outer planet) is somewhat the same as comparing a marble to a basketball. Thus, the outer planets are quite larger, contain considerable more mass, and move much slower than the inner planets. From an astrological point of view, the outer planets seem to exert influence over long-range trends and extended cycles, while the inner planets (because of their speed and proximity and smaller size) seem to influence the more mundane day-to-day activities that we experience.

In this sense, the inner planets are called "the personal planets," while the outer planets are called "the universal planets." On one level of consciousness, we experience our very intimate private existence. On another, we experience what all mankind understands. There is a difference between what an individual sees as personal and what he understands as experiences that he shares with his entire species.

Perhaps the most fascinating difference between the inner and outer planets occurs through each inner planet holding rulership over two zodiac signs while each of the outer planets rules one. The double rulerships of the inner planets involve both a masculine and a feminine sign. Thus, Mercury is the masculine ruler of Gemini and the feminine ruler of Virgo. Venus is the feminine ruler of Taurus and the masculine ruler of Libra. And, Mars, is the masculine ruler of Aries and the feminine ruler of Scorpio. What we see here is the yin and yang, positive-negative dualities that exist on a personal level. Man often experiences "double-mindedness" in his opinions, decisions, sexual differences and attitudes. The outer planets (each ruling only one sign) symbolize the "one-mindedness" of Universal Truth. Thus, there are two distinctly unique experiences for man. One is the duality of his personal life and the other is his more complete understanding of the *one reality* that exists for everybody.

What is extremely interesting is to discover that these

inner and outer planet rulerships actually form a very distinct pattern.

Spring (Aries, Taurus and Gemini) is ruled by the inner planets, Mars, Venus and Mercury. When summer ends and fall begins (Virgo, Libra and Scorpio) the rulership of these three inner planets appears again, but now in exactly the reverse order (Mercury, Venus, and Mars). Spring develops as these planets move in the direction of the Sun. When summer turns to fall, these same planets move in the direction away from the Sun. This analogy seems to break down in terms of Mars, Venus and Mercury having direct rulership over the spring season, but when the process reverses itself it does not begin exactly at fall. Instead, it starts one month earlier in Virgo (Mercury) at the end of the summer. It almost seems as if the reversal is premature and should begin one sign later under the Cardinal quality of Libra. What is really happening here is that the two signs Cancer and Leo ruled respectively by the Moon and Sun are at the exact center of this Inner Planet reversal.

1	2	3	4	5	6	7	8
Aries	Taurus	Gemini	Cancer	Leo	Virgo	Libra	Scorpio
ruled by	ruled by	ruled by	ruled by	ruled by	ruled by	ruled by	ruled by
Mars →	Venus →	Mercury →	Moon	Sun	← Mercury	← Venus	← Mars ←(Pluto)

The two Luminaries or two Lights (Sun and Moon) are at the center of personal fulfillment. Looking at the above diagram from both extremes we find Mars (sexual activity) moving inward to Venus (love) moving further inward to Mercury (understanding) and culminating from both directions at the Sun and the Moon,—the center of the Day and Night of creation and symbolizing Mother and Father as the origin and source of the "family unit."

The outer planets, Jupiter, Saturn, Uranus and Neptune are not focused towards fulfillment within a personalized family structure, but rather towards the understanding of a cooperative world family that functions through a Divine harmony. Pluto, being the outermost known planet serves two functions. As the last of the outer planets it symbolizes world transformation. But, at the same time it is the co-ruler of Scorpio and with Mars also has a function in regards to the family structure. Thus, we see how individuals on a personal level learn how to transform themselves, often transcending family ties in order to seek a greater fulfillment in the outside world.

What really occurs in Scorpio, as we can see in the diagram, is the manifestation of a double purpose. Mars as it is expressed through the conscious use of energy is directed back towards the family structure, while Pluto (which symbolizes the unconscious energies of universal thought) is directed towards the outside world. This is the reason why Scorpio as a sign represents so much upheaval. The combination of these two planets shows the ways in which the individual strives to be a part of a greater individuality as they struggle to express their own uniqueness within their family structure. Thus, the ways in which an individual believes they are expressing their own independence and originality through Mars is really on an unconscious level the ways in which they symbolically represent the free and independent will of mankind as a race.

When we think of the outer planets in order, they show us the distinct ways a person becomes aware of his cosmic role in the grand plan for man. Moving progressively outward from the Sun, Jupiter, Saturn, Uranus, Neptune and Pluto, symbolize the sequential ways of understanding the larger and deeper things that life on a universal level is made of. Still, these planets bear relationships with the inner planets. They express the higher octaves or impersonal goals of what the inner planets perceive personally. Thus, we might extend our diagram in this way.

Where Mars-ruled Aries shows the personal expression of desire, the Pluto rulership of Scorpio represents the unconscious thrust of humanity's desire for transformation. Thus, Pluto symbolizes the universal expression of Mars. As such, we call it the higher octave of Mars. Neptune

INNER PLANETS

Aries	Taurus	Gemini	Cancer	Leo	Virgo	Libra	Scorpio
ruled by	ruled by	ruled by	ruled by	ruled by	ruled by	ruled by	ruled by
Mars	Venus	Mercury	Moon	Sun	Mercury	Venus	Mars

FIND COSMIC EXPRESSION THROUGH
OUTER PLANETS

Scorpio	Pisces	Aquarius	Capricorn	Sagittarius
ruled by	ruled by	ruled by	ruled by	ruled by
Pluto	Neptune	Uranus	Saturn	Jupiter

symbolizes the significant compassion, sacrifice and silent caring that is the higher octave of Venus' love. Uranus represents the enlightened intellect that sparkles with originality and genius. Thus, it manifests the higher octave of Mercury's ability to think and concentrate. In essence, it gives the mind the interest to focus on a universal level.

Saturn has never traditionally been established as the higher octave of any inner planet. But, it does bear a very strong relationship with the Moon. As the ruler of Capricorn, Saturn represents the fulfilled results of what is emotionally started by the Moon. Thus, we can see the nature of karma (i.e. causes through the Moon followed by results through Saturn) in these two planets. As the Moon through its rulership over birth and the beginnings of things symbolizes origins, Saturn shows the concrete form that manifests as these origins mature to fruition. As a result, where the Moon rules individual emotions, it is the collected results of many individuals' emotions which together show the structured form of society (Saturn's effect).

Jupiter also has not been traditionally established as the higher octave of any inner planet. But, it does have a very strong relationship to the Sun. Aside from being the largest planet in our solar system, Jupiter bears the strange characteristic of emitting more energy than it receives. According to the basic definition of what a planet is and what a Sun is, Jupiter then carries with it some Sun-like characteristics. Thus, in a way, we can almost consider it to be a second Sun in our solar system. Where the true Sun holds rulership over the Self as one's center of being, Jupiter signifies the resurrected spirit of the higher mind. Through this, man understands his place in the universe, not on a personal level, but rather through his ability to see and understand universal wisdom. When he can do this, he can expand his consciousness and experience the true fullness of life.

What is extremely interesting is that the diagram shows no connection between the signs, Virgo, Libra, and Scorpio and any of the outer-planet ruled signs. Venus is the positive ruler of Libra and the negative ruler of Taurus. Traditionally, it has been considered to express its quality of love more graciously through Libra and more earthly through Taurus. But, Libra because it is a positive sign is in basic contradiction to the energies of negative Venus. Through its receptive polarity, this planet in Taurus is more sensitized to all of the qualities of earthly love. Some astrologers may feel that Libra is the most natural expression of Venus, and that Neptune as the ruler of Pisces really is the higher octave of Venus as Libra's ruler. If this controversy is to ever be resolved, perhaps the best way of looking at it is that Neptune as the ruler of Pisces symbolizes the water that molds and actually changes the shape of the earth (through its lower octave rulership of Venus in Taurus). If Venus in Libra is the lower octave of Neptune's rulership of Pisces, then we can understand this relationship as water adding its moisture to air (Libra). Thus, the effect becomes somewhat of a stream of thought or consciousness. Mankind actually needs both. The real physical world (Taurus) is where one actually learns the quality of love. In Libra the thoughts or consciousness of love are more important. In either case, however, Neptune shows the ability to bring love (be it in action or consciousness) to a higher form of expression.

We can use this same analogy between Mercury's role in Gemini and in Virgo. Mercury is the true ruler of Gemini while it is exalted in Virgo. But, whether it is more important for us to distinguish between these two signs on this basis or to see the difference in the two different ways the planet actually works, will lead us to different conclusions. Rather than being concerned between the mute difference that exists in our definition of rulership and exaltation, we can understand the lower and higher octave relationship clearer by realizing that Gemini is an air sign and Virgo is an earth sign. In Gemini, Mercury's quality of understanding is applied through thought. In Virgo, Mercury's ability to reason helps to establish a sense of order in the world of things. Thus, Uranus (which stimulates the intellect) symbolizes the changing and growing conscious mind if we see it as the higher octave of Mercury's rulership in Gemini for it shows how the dualities of man's lower or mundane mind find better expression as these inconsistancies are measured against universal mind. If we see Uranus as the higher octave of Mercury's exaltation in Virgo, then the relationship between these two planets becomes one of how man's higher intellect teaches him how to improve and perfect the ways in which he perceives his environment. Again, we have the situation which in either case shows how Uranus symbolizes the ways in which Mercury finds its higher expression.

In the diagram, we also see the sign Scorpio appearing twice; first under the inner-planetary rulership of Mars and secondly under the outer-planetary rulership of Pluto. Thus, the sign acts as a bridge between man's personal efforts at expressing himself and the symbolic ways in which he is an integral part of mass consciousness; which is forever unfolding into new and unknown areas.

Retrograde Motion

At different times during the year, as the planets move along their path around the Sun, they sometimes slow down enough for earth to pass them. When this occurs, they appear to be moving backwards; even though their true direction of movement is unaltered. When this occurs, the planet or planets involved are in "apparent" Retrograde motion. All of the planets except for the Sun and the Moon can at different times appear in Retrograde motion. The interesting thing about this phenomenon is the unexpected results and effects of these changes in planetary motion, as we experience such effects here on earth.

When a planet appears in Retrograde motion, we tend to experience the effects of that planet in inverse and disproportionate ways. For example, Mercury, which symbolizes communication and man's need for understanding tends to make communication difficult when it appears in Retrograde motion. Venus, the planet of love tends to make the experiencing of love difficult when it appears retrograde.

One might assume that planets in Retrograde motion have a tendency to create opposite effects of planets in direct motion. Often, this is so, but usually, the effects of retrograde motion planets are felt far deeper and on much more significant levels. The retrograde Venus, for example, could bring an individual much more in touch with their inner love nature. Thus, they might have difficulty expressing their feelings outwardly, but they might nevertheless experience love with much more depth.

The inner planets (Mercury, Venus, Mars) experience short periods of retrogradation; sometimes several weeks to several months at a time. The outer planets, however, (Jupiter, Saturn, Uranus, Neptune and Pluto) experience much longer periods of retrograde motion; sometimes several months to almost a year at a time. Thus, when we experience the specific effects of inner planets in retrograde motion, we go through changes in our daily lives on a basic level. But, when outer planets are retrograde, the world we live in experiences events and changes in consciousness on a much more universal level. Since the time period of retrogradation is longer, these outer planetary apparent changes in motion signify long range changes in trends, directions, and different perceptions of the ways in which we view our lives.

According to the nature of the planet involved, there is a tendency for its retrograde motion to reverse the natural progressive effect of the planet moving in direct motion. Thus, we often have to retrace our steps during periods of retrogradation in order to re-evaluate, and take a second look at the direction our actions have been moving in when the planet had been in direct motion. Sometimes, this is experienced as a period of stagnation, or a temporary monotonous "waiting" for a sense of forward movement to reappear. But, in reality, it affords us time to realize in consciousness, the effects of things we may have only skimmed over at first glance. thus, Retrograde motion becomes important to observe if we are to understand the reasons why our lives do not always appear to have the simplistic order or consistency that we might otherwise expect.*

---

*See, *Karmic Astrology Volume II-Retrogrades and Reincarnation*, by Martin Schulman, published by Samuel Weiser Inc. New York, 1977

Rulership, Exaltation, Detriment, Fall

*T*he Ancients who studied astrology gave much attention to the elements. Knowing a great deal about the science (even in those times) they were able to devise a method of understanding the planets according to these elements.

During the course of the year the planets move through the different zodiac signs, unemotionally fulfilling their orbits. Nevertheless, four important placements were discovered in which the planets exhibited very unique properties. The Ancients described these special placements with the words, "rulership," "exaltation," "detriment," and "fall."

To see how these four conditions were arrived at, we might ask the question, "How could one describe the Sun (the light and heat which is basically stationary at the center of our solar system) in terms of the elements?" Obviously, the categorization that best fits it, is Fixed-Fire. Then, from this categorization what zodiac sign best fits the mode-element description? This leads us to Leo (the fixed-fire sign). Therefore, we call the Sun the ruler of the sign, Leo.

The Moon which rules the tides, and through whose movement the initiatory changes in water (fluids) including the twenty eight day female menstrual cycle is influenced is best described by the designation of Cardinal-Water. The zodiac sign that is most suitable to this Cardinal-Water description is Cancer (the waters of birth that initiate summer).

In this manner, each planet has a mode-element description which fits with a particular zodiac sign. Thus, a planet's best harmony with the quality of a sign is given the title of "Rulership." It only stands to reason that exactly six months later when the planet is in the sign opposite where it holds rulership that it is "out of season." Thus, the mode-element qualities that put the planet and the sign enough in harmony with each other to be designated as rulership, then experience an opposing quality which the Ancients called "Detriment." A planet is always in its detriment when it is found in the sign opposite where it rules.

The Ancients also observed that each planet had more than a single quality. The sun is fixed at the center of our solar system, but because of its brilliance and power, it is able to initiate activity throughout the solar system. Thus, it also has a cardinal initatory quality to it. And, it is through this cardinal initiatory quality that the Sun finds its exaltation in the cardinal sign, Aries. The Moon, whose basic quality is cardinal, continues along a fixed path around the earth. While it effects changes in the tides, these changes are fixed in their timing and quite accurately predictable. Thus, there is a constant quality to the Moon in addition to its cardinal characteristics. And, it is through this fixed or constant nature that the Moon finds its exaltation in the fixed sign, Taurus. The sign in which a planet exhibits its second most harmonious quality is called, "exaltation." Sometimes this is found through the element and sometimes through the mode. The Ancients used the word, exaltation to describe the sign in which a planet is enhanced, developed and augmented. Thus, although a planet in its exaltation is not in its true home (or rulership), it nevertheless receives enough help from the sign to function in a positive and expansive manner.

When a planet appears in the sign opposite where it is exalted, it finds interference with its free expression. As a result, this effect usually manifests through difficulties in that area of life which the planet represents. Traditionally, this has been defined as a planet in its fall.

The fixed quality of the Moon's ever-constant orbit around the earth allows the sign Taurus (which astrologers are beginning to suspect may well be ruled by earth itself) to enhance and exalt the Moon's receptive and nourishing qualities. But, when the Moon appears in Scorpio (opposite Taurus, where it is exalted) the volatile upheavals of Scorpio become too disruptive for the Moon to truly exhibit its nourishing essence.

In the diagram we see the established rulership, exaltation, detriment and fall of all the planets. The specific exaltation and fall for Pluto (the last planet to be discovered) has not yet been established.

Notice that neither the Sun or the Moon hold rulership, exaltation, detriment or fall in any mutable sign. This mode then, is not part of the four different special qualities that the luminaries can experience.

If we look at the elements, we find that in the four special placements for the Sun, the Earth and Water qualities are missing. The Moon compliments the Sun by finding its special placement in Earth and Water signs instead of the Fire and Air elements. Mercury balances out the Sun and the Moon by exhibiting itself through four signs which represent all the elements.

From Venus on outward, the system lacks equal representation of modes and elements. Perhaps one of the reasons is that there may well be planets we have not yet discovered that fit these missing modes and elements.

Something else very interesting shows up if we study the "Rulership" column in the diagram. Imagining the Asteroid Belt as an unknown planet that either could not form or was somehow destroyed by forces we are not

PLANET	RULERSHIP	EXALTATION	DETRIMENT	FALL
SUN	LEO Fixed Fire	ARIES Cardinal Fire	AQUARIUS Fixed Air	LIBRA Cardinal Air
MOON	CANCER Cardinal Water	TAURUS Fixed Earth	CAPRICORN Cardinal Earth	SCORPIO Fixed Water
MERCURY	GEMINI Mutable Air	VIRGO Mutable Earth	SAGITTARIUS Mutable Fire	PISCES Mutable Water
VENUS	LIBRA Cardinal Air	PISCES Mutable Water	ARIES Cardinal Fire	VIRGO Mutable Earth
MARS	ARIES Cardinal Fire	CAPRICORN Cardinal Earth	LIBRA Cardinal Air	CANCER Cardinal Water
JUPITER	SAGITTARIUS Mutable Fire	CANCER Cardinal Water	GEMINI Mutable Air	CAPRICORN Cardinal Earth
SATURN	CAPRICORN Cardinal Earth	LIBRA Cardinal Air	CANCER Cardinal Water	ARIES Cardinal Fire
URANUS	AQUARIUS Fixed Air	SCORPIO Fixed Water	LEO Fixed Fire	TAURUS Fixed Earth
NEPTUNE	PISCES Mutable Water	LEO Fixed Fire	VIRGO Mutable Earth	AQUARIUS Fixed Air
PLUTO	SCORPIO Fixed Water		TAURUS Fixed Earth	

*(Students will find different tables of rulerships available. As they study, they will determine the validity of each.)

familiar with, consider the position between Mars and Jupiter (where this Asteroid Belt is) as a starting point. Consider also that Venus is not only the Ruler of Libra, but also the ruler of Taurus. Now starting from Mars read the Rulership column going upward. You will observe that by substituting Taurus for Libra, the zodiac signs appear in their correct order as the Inner Planets move in the direction of the Sun.

Taking the same Rulership column, now read it downward from Jupiter's rulership of Sagittarius. You will notice that as the planets move in the direction away from the Sun, the signs again follow in the correct order, but this time with one exception. Could Scorpio (the sign of endings) really be the last sign of the zodiac in some mystical way that we are not aware of?

The entire concept of Rulership, Exaltation, Detriment and Fall is filled with mystery. It leaves much for the student to ponder on in terms of what did the Ancients know that we do not? Still, on a much lighter level, our ability to categorize the planets and signs in this manner helps us to understand the natural qualities that occur when different elements combine with each other. And, this gives us a much fuller understanding of what the planets and signs really mean.

If one wishes to pursue the mystery, the question might be asked, why is no planet exalted in the sign Gemini (the sign of cleavage, mitosis, and atom-splitting)? Could this have something to do with the Asteroid Belt we know so little about? What is the true mystical ruler of Virgo, or are the virtuous ideals of this sign beyond comprehension to mortal man? Some of nature is seen and some of nature is unseen. The system for planetary rulership, exaltation, detriment, and fall is based on both.

For the convenience of interpretation, planets in rulership or exaltation add harmony to the horoscope by working easily for the individual in those areas of his life that they represent. At the same time, planets in detriment

SPRING			SUMMER			FALL			WINTER		
Mars	Venus	Mercury	Moon	Sun	Mercury	Venus	Mars & Pluto	Jupiter	Saturn	Uranus	Neptune
♈	♉	♊	♋	♌	♍	♎	♏	♐	♑	♒	♓
The beginning (oneness, self)	Constancy, tangibility, fact	Relationship, communication duality,	Birth (Nourishment)	Growth (abundance of blessings) achievement, power, control	Organization, understanding of virtue and perfect order	True love, harmony, balance	Sexual fulfillment, transformations	Knowledge, fortune, expansion, freedom	Wisdom, tradition, practicality, foresight	Discovery, invention, evolution	Receiving the Divine nature, compassion sacrifice, cosmic understanding

and fall are testing grounds through which an individual must learn how to accept and understand the seeming paradoxes that are still a part of nature's way.

When we look at the seasons and the sequence of signs, the concept of planetary rulership shows a definite progression according to Cosmic Law. What the Ancients have not told us we may be able to understand from the essence of nature herself.

The Planets and their Meaning

*P*lanets are alive. They move, they have specific properties, they emit different types of energies, and they have particular effects upon the earth. To build a firm astrological foundation we need to gain a thorough understanding of their symbolism. When we understand these meanings then the rest of astrology becomes incredibly simple! The student who only memorizes planetary meanings, but does not know why they mean what they do is not building a good foundation for solid astrological thinking. One cannot form good sentences before understanding what the words mean. In essence then, there is a sequence to the building of an astrological mind.

It has been discovered through observation and empirical research that each planet emanates a different type of energy because of its size, shape, orbit, speed of revolution and the nature of its elemental makeup. We could say that energy moves in rays, much like the rays of the Sun. As these rays strike the Earth, they impart their particular flavor and because we live on Earth, we are able to experience these different kinds of energies. What is important to understand is that although they effect us, they do not rule our lives. We experience the rays, but we can choose different ways of reacting to them. For example, a ray from Jupiter (the planet of happiness) is always shining towards the Earth. Some of us are able to experience it a great deal of the time. some of us never notice that it exists. Some of us believe that the Sun isn't shining on cloudy days; forgetting completely that the Sun shines beyond the clouds that hide it.

The planets symbolize a wide variety of energies through which we can experience many different things. But, they don't create for us. It is up to man to know how to experience life so that he can recognize the harmonious flow of planetary energies and learn how to use them to benefit himself and mankind.

The Sun

The Sun is the center of our solar system. It is the central focus of nature's efforts. As the ruler of the sign, Leo, it's extreme brilliance symbolizes the middle of summer when all of nature proudly displays her beauty. the blossoms open revealing their vivid colors. All plant life has abundant foliage and the rich fragrance of vital energy. Animal life scurries everywhere enjoying the warmth of the Sun's healing rays. At this time of the year the earth is close to the Sun and readily able to receive all the bounty it has to offer. We feel this as our entire system becomes more vibrant. We experience a strong sense of vitality which adds inspiration to creative ideas. We take pride in all we have accomplished as we begin to sense a greater Divine potential in life.

The Sun holds rulership over the center of one's being. All else revolves around this. It is the primary "light" that attracts everything to it, and from which ultimately emanates all that an individual thinks, feels and does. In midsummer the plant reveals a purpose which could hardly be detected in the seeds of early spring; so too, man finds his purpose from the warmth of the Sun's rays. There is a quality of royal splendor in the Sun: a spendor that gives man his vital life force, and shows him the best ways in which to use it.

The Sun gives individuals hope by adding brigh†ness to their lives. Traditionally the realm of emotions has been ascribed to the Moon, however, if we look at nature we discover that this is not entirely so. On dismal days when the Sun is not readily visible, one's entire emotional outlook tends to lack the vibrant quality that is present on sunny days. Conversely, Sunlight can be used as a cure for emotional depression, lethargy in animals, and wilting plants. The greatest changes in one's spiritual outlook are affected through the amount of light one can perceive. "God created the heavens and earth." The strongest perceivable light in the heavens is unquestionably the Sun. Thus, for man it symbolizes many of the celestial qualities that he can absorb into his being.

The Sun symbolizes strength, a centered outlook, the power of being, the source of one's creative output. The quality of the constellation or zodiac sign that the Sun is in at birth shows the principle quality through which an individual can be most in harmony with himself through life.

As the Sun moves through the twelve signs of the zodiac, the earth absorbs twelve different but equally important qualities. Whatever an individual's Sun sign is, by living it to its fullest potential he can symbolize on earth one twelfth of God's complete plan for life. an individual's Sun sign represents his center of energy; his primary source of life.

The sun is always low on the horizon in the morning, high in the sky at midday and low on the horizon again in late afternoon. It is interesting to note how some people find it difficult to wake in the morning, are highly active by midday and fairly tired by late afternoon. Thus we can see how the world adjusts itself to the energy it feels from the Sun.

Taking this same analogy and expanding it, one can readily understand why individuals cannot realize the full potential of their Sun sign until mid-life. The Sun rules both opportunity and realization, the two qualities which when combined can bring a person to self-mastery.

An individual's Sun sign is his most natural way of being unique. It shows his approach to life and the way he perceives himself as well as how he perceives all that is around him. The world exists in an objective sense. A river flows because it does. That is its nature. Each Sun sign will perceive the river differently. One will see it as a means of travel. Another will see the water as useful for washing. another may think of it as the baptism of the earth. Still another is attracted to its texture and color. And still another sees it as an environment for aquatic life. The river is all of these things and more.

A tree grows because it does. One Sun sign will admire the beauty of the tree and its shape and colors. Another will tend to be more concerned with its useful function to man. Another will wonder at its size and placement. Another will hardly notice it at all.

The Sun symbolizes the objective light of reality perceived differently from different angles. It has the element of Fire which creates activity. Man learns to harness the fire within himself so he can focus his activities in order to realize the full potential of his being.

In nature, there is enough Sunlight for all of creation. Every tree, plant, flower, and animal has its niche. Each fulfills its purpose in its season. And each receives exactly enough Sunlight to reach its purpose. When man is unwilling to absorb and use the power, strength and energy that the Sun is giving him, he may not realize his purpose. He looks to others for purpose and begins imitating all that he cannot be, while avoiding all that he can be. The great Chinese sage, Lao Tsu said, "Three in ten are followers of life." The individual who understands the opportunity symbolized by the Sun is able to become one of these "three in ten."

It is so obvious why many ancient societies worshipped the Sun. They felt its generous giving nature as the source of all of their crops, the strength of their livestock, and the perpetuation of one season after another. They never doubted the Sun's ability to shine with the coming of each new day. From this faith, they developed hope and faith in themselves. They were able to sense a continuity to their lives and ultimately realize a reason for their existence. Although we do not create gods for the Sun today, we do understand it as a part of the living God's plan for us. From this understanding, we can realize that the Sun symbolizes mid-day, "the light", the center of one's being. The Sun symbolizes the objective power of reality in whose framework we may create our lives.

KEYWORDS:

Brilliance, vividness, vitality, light, Father, generosity, opportunity, fulfillment, source, center of being, life, independence, popularity, strength, power, enlightment, expansiveness, assertiveness, pride, leadership, cheeriness, wealth, attractiveness, creativity, conscious existence, rules the fifth year of anything, procreation.

Planetary Hours: One O'clock, Ten O'clock
Day of the Week: Sunday
Traverses a Sign: 1 month
Rules: Leo

The Moon

The Moon is the other luminary. Having no light of its own, it reflects the light of the Sun and holds rulership over the "night" of creation. Its influence is felt strongest in the sign Cancer, when nature is nourishing itself in the direction of fulfillment. It is interesting to note that photosynthesis (the process through which all plant life grows) takes place only at night.

Where the Sun holds rulership over all that shows its brilliance, the Moon holds rulership over all which must be deeply looked through in order to see brilliance. Thus, the area of human emotion has been traditionally allocated to the Moon. Emotions are fluid in nature, and while they often do not show the "truth," they are the path to it!

Where the Sun symbolizes the masculine-dominant nature of fulfillment in midsummer, the Moon represents the nourishing process of early summer that leads to it. It is receptively feminine in its gentle flowing quality. It symbolizes all in nature that bends and yields; that which is soft and pliable, and capable of reflecting the rays of the Sun. The Moon is the receiver and carrying womb of that which is to be used in the birth process. It takes exactly twenty eight days for the Moon to complete its cycle through the twelve zodiac signs, coinciding with the female menstrual cycle!

The Sun is that part of a tree which stands tall, the Moon is the gentle colorful beauty of the leaves, the stamen in the flowers, and the seeds within the fruit. Earth needs feelings to come alive. The Moon supplies the different tones, colors, essences and fragrances that create these feelings. The Sun supplies the energy for creation. The Moon has a strong influence over creativity as well, particularly in the areas of art, poetry, music, dance and all activities where we express our feelings about the environment in which we live.

The Moon expresses the Water element. The human body is ninety percent water. A great portion of the earth's surface is also water. It is the running sap of life, the current of nourishment.

A forest survives better than a single tree. As the great poet, Kahlil Gibran put it, "When the lions roar their presence, the Forest does not feel dismay." Flowers grow in bunches, birds fly in flocks, and animals travel in packs. Man, too, has found through the ages that he grows stronger in numbers of his own kind. The concept of family has evolved since antiquity and continues to be that natural part of life through which one gains sustenance and nourishment. Like the forest, the flock of birds, the pack of animals, even schools of fish, "family" is that protective insulating buffer that helps man to grow stronger while coping with his environment. The family is ruled by the Moon in its nourishing, mothering qualities.

Where the Sun says, "I am," the Moon says "I feel." Individuals first learn about their feelings in the family setting. During the preschool years the Moon is a dominating force in a child's life. In nearly all species of animal life, the young learn about mother love before thay are capable of transferring their feelings. The word "feelings" is broad because it includes instincts, hunches, intuitions, silent knowings that come from the Moon's vibration. The quality of E.S.P. that exists in humans as well as in plants and animals is symbolized by the Moon. Public opinion, the plural of individual feelings is also under the influence of the Moon. Nature itself is envisioned as "Mother Nature," or in Eastern philosophy as the "Divine Mother."

Why do we always feel more romantic in moonlight? Why does the day more easily lend itself to work, while the night seems to blend with feelings? Why do individuals feel more emoting qualities with eyes closed? The light reflected from the Moon balances the direct sunlight during day. It has a different quality to it. Where the direct sunlight shows everything in its most vivid brilliance, often too dazzling to look at, the moonlight has a gentle, softening quality. It receives the light of the Sun and feeds it to the Earth at night. It is the Universal Mother receiving the male principle and feeding her young from all she reflects.

The Moon rules all foods and the caring that they represent. Food can be in physical form, or in the form of ideas and thoughts which help to nourish the ways in which an individual grows. Domesticity, protectiveness, anything in nature which symbolizes an extension of the womb and the ability to shield is under the Moon's influence. The interior of a home with all that makes it cozy, warm and protective shows this quality. Within the home we establish our safety and nourish ourselves with all that we need to meet the outside world.

Since the Moon symbolizes reflection, it also holds rulership over memory; that quality which remembers the Sun. Memory is the recollection of that which was received at an earlier time. The Moon helps the earth retain the memory of the Sun's light even when it is not receiving it directly. In like manner, memory is the retaining womb of all feelings, as it unconsciously contains all that an individual has experienced.

KEYWORDS:

Emotions, impressions, intuition, Mother, creativity, compassion, insight, reflection, mirrors, gardening, plants, foods, nourishments, birth, the womb, sexual feeling, female menstrual cycle, tides, opening of oysters, the body, stomach and breasts, preschool years, receptivity, sensitivity, E.S.P., fluids, moods, memory, night, emotional foundations, home, domesticity, tree sap, sewing, knitting, cooking, real estate, the roots of the soul, the public, the uncouscious, rules the fourth year of everything.

Planetary Hour: Two o'clock
Day of the Week: Monday
Traverses a Sign: 2¼ days
Rules: Cancer

Mercury

Mercury is the closest planet to the Sun. It rules Gemini (the changing of spring to summer) and Virgo (the changing of summer to fall). In both instances it rules the last sign of a season, where the experiences of the season are brought to culmination and understood through the mind.

This is the planet of understanding. Its action creates change through thought. We can readily see how important this is if we realize that it is conscious thought that sets man above the rest of nature. He has the ability to reason, and the more he uses this ability the more he is able to focus himself in the "Now" of his existence. Man is what he perceives. Through the Moon he receives unconscious impressions, but through Mercury he learns how to refine his five conscious senses so that he can achieve optimum functionability in his life.

This is the only personal planet that is dispassionate. Therefore it symbolizes our ability to make the correct choices in our personal life without being confused by emotions or sensitivities that could lure us in directions that are unreasonable. Both Gemini and Virgo represent activity in a mundane sense. Mercury (activated by its closeness to the Sun) enables an individual to focus on all the small details that make up his life. Thus, we are able to balance our feelings with what we think.

Because Mercury rules two signs on either side of Cancer and Leo, this very special planet shows how we can center the Self in the direction of the two luminaries (Sun and Moon) through conscious understanding. We communicate through Mercury (as the ruler of Gemini) all that we feel (Cancer). But, we also do (Mercury's rulership of Virgo) the things which express all we are (Leo). Our humane relationships (Gemini) help us test our feelings (Cancer), and our relationship with all the things in the environment (Virgo) help us to establish what we are (Leo).

Mercury influences the early school years where an individual first becomes acquainted with the thinking process separate and apart from his parents. During these early years an individual first develops platonic friendships. He learns the value of discussing ideas with others, and

Independent Thought	P A R E N T S		Independent Thought
Gemini	Cancer	Leo	Virgo
ruled by Mercury	ruled by Moon	ruled by Sun	ruled by Mercury

develops an inquisitive mind seeking to understand all the things in the world that he is just beginning to perceive. At this age, a child begins to make short trips from home without his parents' guidance. All of these things come under Mercury's domain.

Mercury, the winged messenger of the Gods in myths, serves humanity through communication. Everything necessary for self-expression is ruled by this planet. Writing implements (pens, pencils, stationary, typewriters, blackboards, chalk, erasers), as well as speaking implements (telephones, microphones), communication devices (cablegrams, codes, crossword puzzles, anagrams, checkbooks) are all under Mercury's rulership. We use messenger services, we take short journeys, we attend meetings and the like. We learn about our world through newspapers, magazines, books, ledgers and the written word. All that promotes learning is Mercury-ruled.

The earliest writings were done on rocks. The Ten Commandments were received on tablets of stone. Hieroglyphics were carved in caves, buildings and pyramids. In every civilization, man attempted to record his message for future generations. The words of a culture or a society, no matter how philosophical they may be, must somehow be communicated through Mercury. The busy quality of cities where minds are active as opposed to the musing quality of rural country areas is strongly indicative of Mercury's great sense of presence.

When man cannot communicate, he becomes asocial. When he cannot express his thoughts he feels atypical. When he cannot learn, he starts to believe that somehow the world is passing him by. Thus, Mercury's need to express, communicate and learn is extremely important for the growth and development of each individual. It is through Mercury that man slowly builds a mental filtering mechanism which brings into his life all that he needs while screening out all that is unnecessary. Success in small matters is the fulfillment that Mercury offers.

Mercury also symbolizes coordination between mind and hands: Repairing machinery, mechanical aptitude, manual dexterity, cleaning, organizing and understanding. We can hear Mercury in the sights and sounds around us. We can see it in the movement of people and objects, and we can know it through the intelligence we gain through books and learning. It is this ever-busy intelligence that we call the domain of the conscious mind. And, in this domain the principle purpose of Mercury is to teach an individual how to experience *interest* in himself and the world around him. The word "interest" is not to be taken lightly; for it is a precious commodity through which man can relate to humanity and his environment in ways that make him understand that he is an integrated, functioning part of all he consciously perceives.

KEYWORDS:

Communication, transportation, learning ability, interest, conscious mind, platonic friendships, mental focus, busyness, relatives, implements necessary to communicate, schools, short journeys, the five senses, understanding, the microcosm, attention to details, vivid sense of presence, early school years, mathematics, handwriting, integration, personal objectivity, agility, rules the nervous system, rules the third and sixth year of anything, reason and logic, optimum functioning ability, non-emotional, seeks to understand relationships, siblings, family communication, symbolizes the humaneness of society.

Planetary Hour: Seven o'clock
Day of the Week: Wednesday
Traverses a Sign: 20 days
Rules: Gemini
Exaltation: Virgo

Venus

Venus is the planet of love. It rules the sign Taurus which signifies the beauty of the gentle northern spring soil receiving nature's seeds, as well as the sign Libra, where nature balances herself by turning around her cycle and giving back her gifts. The pure essence of love is found in harmony, cooperation, and the gentle unity between man and his environment.

As the ruler of the earth sign Taurus, Venus symbolizes this harmony in a physical way as the seed combines with the earth for the expectation of future birth. The holiday, "Mother's Day" falling at this time of the year represents the gift of fertility. The Taurean symbol of the Bull is still another manifestation of Venus' fertility rites.

As the ruler of the air sign Libra, Venus points to a different kind of love. The Libra symbol ♎ stands for the setting Sun, which represents the peace man feels after quieting down from the over-activity of summer which precedes it. Here the balance of nature is achieved as the waxing and waning seasons both meet at the center of the zodiac. The love of Libra selflessly sacrifices the visible bounty of the Earth through harvest, rewarding man for his efforts.

Since Taurus is a feminine sign and Libra a masculine sign, it becomes easy to understand that love is truly both feminine and masculine in nature. In Taurus, Venus receives all she can hold. In Libra, Venus gives all she has. This giving is the masculine quality while the receiving is the feminine quality. The fullness of love is an interchange of both.

In the spring, Venus awaits pollination. She expresses her stability and constancy. She is the promise of loyalty and devotion; the provider, the builder of the nest. The earth softens and yields its precious minerals for the abundance that will spring forth from it. In the fall she surrenders her earthly beauty in order to cooperate harmoniously with nature's cycle. She becomes selfless and yet centered.

Venus is the planet of value. All that is precious in man's gentle nature is her domain. Venus symbolizes how life should be, our comforts, our artistic and creative senses, as it softens that which is rough. She smoothes over, soothes, and bathes with love all that is tense and anxious. Rounded shapes, muted and pastel colors, tender forms, and all ways in which we express love come through the Venus energy.

Money is used to attain resources and express values. We buy beautiful things and fulfill our need for sensory pleasure. We possess things as long as they are useful, as the earth possesses the roots of a plant as long as the plant is growing. All that is needed for barter and exchange is a product of Venus. The giving and receiving of gifts is one of the warmest expressions of Venusian love.

As the planet of beauty, Venus rules architecture, design, building and texture. It symbolizes our ability to appreciate love and pleasure. It helps to make us content with our lot in life through the understanding of gratitude. But, it can also make us lazy and complacent. Although Venus holds rulership over all the finer things in life, she is also the planet of balance, proportion and correct perspective. Too much of anything too good tends to become bad (the spiritual lesson of Venus' rulership in Taurus). When beauty and modesty are combined, however, a centered and balanced outlook on life is achieved (the spiritual lesson of Venus' rulership in Libra).

Venus takes away the sharpness of life, replacing it with a slightly dulled, but extremely pleasing conception of things. It rules the feminine principle, particularly younger women and daughters, leaving older females and mothers to the rulership of the Moon. The understanding of emotions usually ascribed to wisdom gained through experience and age comes from the light of the Moon as one of the two luminaries. Venus, in her rulership over younger women, feels emotions and expresses feelings, but does not have the illumination to fully understand them.

Where Mercury holds rulership over the early school years when the thinking processes are being developed, Venus starts to be felt at puberty. Children begin to feel love attractions to members of the opposite sex outside of their family. Exchanges of gifts, greeting cards, love notes are all prevalent during the puberty years. The expression "puppy love" symbolizes still another aspect of Venus' tender caring qualities.

The singing voice that soothes, the hand that reaches out and reassuringly touches, the smile that warms another, colorful gift wrapping paper and designs on glassware and dishes, the embroidery on pillows, wood carvings on furniture, designs on lace tableclothes, parasols, stained glass windows, etchings, colorful lights and candles, flower arrangements, and the harmony in color and texture of clothing are all expressions of the love and beauty of Venus.

Hobbies which require a great deal of care, love and attention are also under the rulership of Venus. Building models, gardening, decorating, working with cermaics, graphics, the shaping and forming of anything that will be pleasing to the eye and gentle to the senses are expressions of Venus' rulership.

To care and to be cared for, to do things that will please another, the act of sharing, and the ability to receive are all ways of feeling love. To go through life being able to be part of another, and allowing another to be part of oneself is perhaps the most intimate expressions of love that exists. Doing with love (Taurus) and thinking with love (Libra) give man his most rewarding experiences. There is no wealth in the world, no fame or glory or riches of any kind that compare to loving and being loved in return. There is no feeling of safety and security that can compare to devotion. And there is no greater reason for living than love!

KEYWORDS:

Love, beauty, harmony, gentleness, soothing, softening, tenderness, the female principle, receptiveness, feeling, colors, tones, texture, sensory pleasures, the aesthetics, poetry, art, music, design, comfort, luxury, money, devotion, caring, attachments, likes, cooperation, sharing, peace, tranquility, constructiveness, creativity, gifts, flowers, holidays, decorating, gardening, roundness in form, rules the second and sixth year of anything, appreciation and gratitude, perfumes, ballet, cosmetics.

Planetary Hour: Three o'clock
Day of the Week: Friday
Traverses a Sign: 1 month
Rules: Taurus, Libra

Mars

Mars is the planet of activity. It rules the sign Aries which symbolizes readying the earth for planting in Spring, and holds co-rulership over the sign Scorpio when all is taken out of the earth during the Fall harvest. Thus, Mars is the activity to begin and the activity to complete what was begun earlier. There is always an instinctual quality to the Martian energy. We plant when it is the time to plant. We reap when it is time to reap. In Spring we instinctively desire to initiate new beginnings. We want to make up for all that we feel we missed as a result of winter's concealment. We experience a new sense of vitality and intuitively become aware of our desire nature. We want to run to meet the world and can barely contain the enthusiasm that was concealed all winter.

When we feel the Mars quality again in the fall through Scorpio, our desire turns to receiving all that the earth has to offer. Again there is an urgency to the quest as we sense that winter is not far off. The Mars influence in Aries is somewhat different than its influence in Scorpio, for in Aries, there is desire to experience all that is new; the need to find the most appropriate places to plant the beginning seeds of the fresh season. In Scorpio, however, there is desire to contain and conceal the bounty of the harvest before the time for reaping is past. Still, through their differences, these two seasons reveal both sides of the basic Mars quality.

Mars reflects itself through two moons—Deimos and Phobos. While the principle characteristic of the planet is to manifest activity, these two moons symbolize opposite kinds of activity. Deimos thrusts towards "demonstrative" outer activity as seen in Aries, while Phobos (linked with the word "Phobia") creates inner or concealed activity as manifest through Scorpio.

Activity is the result of how an individual chooses to use the energy he feels. The energy of Mars is always sharp, explicit and direct. It acts through the mental initiatory beginnings of Aries and the sexual drive in Scorpio.

In Aries the planet expresses all the enthusiasm of the northern spring. It adds a vibrant brilliance to an individual's life as it moves in the direction of fertilizing the earth (in Taurus). In Scorpio, however, (which forms an exact six month opposition to Taurus) Mars always acts in association with Pluto to take out from the earth all that was there. This may well be the reason why so many individuals experience a feeling of losing something after the completion of sexual intercourse (Scorpio) in comparison to the feeling of gaining something through sexual attraction (Aries).*

Throughout the zodiac, Mars symbolizes movement. Ideas, thoughts and feelings are not made manifest until they are acted on. Through action, Mars shows what an individual does with all he thinks and feels. When thoughts and feelings are able to be expressed, creation results. When these two qualities are not able to be expressed, the result may be anger (also a characteristic of Mars). In reality, Anger is a distortion of Mars energy which appears whenever an individual holds back from expressing what he feels.

The activity of "expression" is purely a subjective one. Individuals need to express themselves, not necessarily because they are consciously contributing anything to their race, their peers, or their environment, but just because expressing the self is a natural part of being. A flower grows not to please those who view it, but because it is its nature to do so. When an individual uses Mars energy it may or may not please others. This is not its purpose. Instead, Mars is the impetus to do! And, one cannot *be* without doing. However, one can choose to channel this energy in productive directions, thus combining the need to express with the desire to do that which is useful to oneself and one's society.

There are many extremes in nature. There is the plant that grows quickly and the blossom that opens slowly. Both are in a state of doing. Traditionally, we associate Mars with the plant that grows quickly, but this is only one extreme of the Mars quality. In this extreme, Mars manifests as sharp thorny plants, pointed objects, a sense of quickness, the soldier, the battle, the policeman and fireman, competitiveness, the struggle of ego, and all that reflects man's primitive nature. It is usually seen as a planet of violence,

---

*See, *The Astrology of Sexuality*, M. Schulman, publ. Samuel Weiser Inc.

aggressiveness, and argumentativness. All of this is true, but it is only one expression of the Mars energy.

A weed grows quickly and accomplishes its purpose. A tree grows more slowly while accomplishing still a larger purpose. Some planets move about the sun very rapidly, others move slowly. Even slow movement symbolizes activity! Slow moving activity may ultimately be more meaningful. One individual can do a thousand things in a day, appearing to be Mars-like in his behavior. At the end of the day he may be frustrated because he did not direct his energy where he wanted. Another individual may spend an entire day doing only one thing, but at the end of the day, he may realize that he has directed his energy in a harmonious fashion toward his goal. Here we see the difference between the Mars association with Aries and the Mars association with Scorpio. Aries symbolizes maximum activity measured against maximum time. Because Scorpio senses the end of things, there is a fixed determination to harness energy towards its most meaningful purpose. Aries sees purpose and opportunity everywhere, for it feels the entire season ahead of it.

Energy can be used constructively or destructively. Both have their place in natural law. Energy used to discard that which is no longer useful (Scorpio) is just as important as energy used to seek that which is new (Aries). Thus, the true meaning of Mars is found in how an individual plants the seeds of his life in the Spring and harvests their bounty in the Fall.

Mars rules self-projection, any expression of force, the use of power, the front of anything, train engines, motors, that which expresses drive, aggressive need towards progress, doing, acting, movement, cutting, tearing, verbs, sharp pointed objects, fire, industry, industriousness, proving, athletics, competitiveness, anything which is thin and straight, desire, expressing sexuality, combativeness, and the unification of the ego.

Mars is the point of a pen, the head of a match, the edge of a razor, the horns of a bull, the masculine principle, and all expressions of strength. In effect, it is man's way of impressing his reality into the world he lives in, and taking for himself that which he needs. It is the power of the self in conscious action. Where the need of Venus is to blend with another, the need of Mars is to isolate the self in its unique identity.

KEYWORDS:

Activity, drive, initiative, force, aggressiveness, self-actualization, strength, power, impatience, use of energy, boldness, courage, pioneering spirit, enterprise, doing, acting, performing, spontaneity, bravery, need, desire, sexuality, struggle for survival, drive to surpass, leadership, rules the first and eighth year of anything.

Planetary Hour: Five o'clock
Day of the Week: Tuesday
Traverses a Sign: 2 months
Rules: Aries
Co-rules: Scorpio

JUPITER

Jupiter is the planet of expansion. It rules the sign Sagittarius where the abundance of the fall harvest is divided among the people. The season ends with merriment after reaping all that was planted, nourished and cared for during the fertile growing months. The surrender of autumn into winter is accomplished by spreading the wealth of the harvest and enjoying the feast, always with the sense that the closing quality of winter's barrenness is not far off.

Jupiter rules the higher mind. Where Mercury's rulership of Gemini ends the spring season (lower mind), and Mercury's rulership of Virgo ends the summer season (lower mind seeking perfection), Jupiter's rulership of Sagittarius ends the fall season with man's first awareness of his higher mind. The lower mind is used to function on a mundane level. Jupiter powers the higher mind to make broad decisions, sweeping changes, to expand one's consciousness to the realization that there is more to life than what the lower mind conceives. Jupiter is the first of the outer planets, and symbolizes the first energy that puts man in touch with more than just his intimate personal awareness. The planet is likened to the wisdom of King Solomon, the handed-down knowledge advanced by ancient civilizations, the unspoken understanding of truth as it really is. These are non-personal things, and like the spreading of wealth from the harvest, they are shared by humanity as a whole.

Jupiter is the beneficient giver. It is called the greater fortune, bestowing from nature's unbelievable abundance, wealth, riches, bounty, happiness, enough for everybody. Mercury functions best in city areas because of its constant "busyness" in detailed thought; Jupiter functions best in country or open areas, where it is able to see all the little thoughts as part of a greater whole. Wisdom is the ability to synthesize collected knowledge into sensible integration. Jupiter does this by seeing the whole of something rather than focusing on tiny details.

All that is happy, light, spontaneous, abundant, and carefree is under Jupiter's rulership. Again seeing the analogy of the harvest as the reward for the work of the season, Jupiter holds influence over medals, trophies, honours, receiving abundant gifts, and having more than what was originally expected. It is also the planet of luck, good fortune, lotteries and gambling, gatherings for happy occasions and whatever causes high spirits. Jupiter rules horizons. Man knows what he has and what his life is about, but always envisions something more. He tries to broaden his understanding by learning different philosophies and extending his education. Where Mercury rules lower education, Jupiter gives the opportunity of higher education through colleges, religions, philosophies, libraries, publishers, all ways in which man tries to communicate his more elevated ideas to his fellow man.

Jupiter rules journeys to far distant places and long journeys into the mind; both enable man to broaden his horizons and look at life in a more objective way. As the largest of the planets, it was mythologically called "Jove", the king of the gods; the giving father upon whose abundant generosity all could count on. When the harvest comes, the abundance benefits the farmer as well as those who didn't work! Such is the nature of Jupiter's supreme good fortune.

It rules man-made law, but not cosmic law, for cosmic law is governed by all of the planets. The laws of society, however, are an attempt at achieving truth through wisdom, two of Jupiter's primary qualities.

After man fulfills his personal needs through the inner planets, he seeks a more expansive knowledge of what life is about. He asks "why?," not necessarily for his own personal gain, but because something is prompting him to want to be part of the grand plan. He poses such questions in his mind that cause him to ponder the nature of truth, and he seeks more complete answers rather than just the partial glimpses he gets through Mercury. Why do civilizations rise and fall? What is the nature of right and wrong? What is the true religion? What is happiness? These are the kinds of questions Jupiter asks. And, their answers are not personal, but universal. Man's wisdom is what he can harvest from everyone he knows, everything he can read, every place he can go, and all that he is able to understand as part of nature.

Jupiter is much larger than the other planets, and as such, holds rulership over everything that is big or gradiose. Stately mansions, large Sequioia or Redwood trees, the Grand Canyon, the Sahara desert, large fortunes, are all manifestations of Jupiter's abundance. From so much, one gains a sense of freedom from the mundane. There is a releasing of trivial thought and attachment to minituae in order to appreciate the bountiful spirit of life that is present everywhere. Through this planet, opportunity exists for all. Nature in its wildest forms shows the pure expression of Jupiter's abundant expansiveness. The planet holds rulership over large undomesticated animals. Their freedom of spirit and thirst for life is such an integrated part of God's plan that one need only corral a wild stallion and watch its disappointment to understand that all life is intended to be free. The essence of optimism, hope, zest, vitality, and generosity is based on freedom of expression. Rules and discipline are necessary only when love is absent. Thus, the love that nature exhudes in her unfailing abundance is a result of her freedom to give it. Were she too confined, her spirit of happiness, cheerfulness, and generosit would be unduly stifled, and the bigness of nature that makes us in awe of its wonders would be denied.

There is a spontaneity to Jupiter's vibration that does not hold back anything. It flows like a great river, pours like a stream and grows like the millions of branches on every tree. Nature's bounty gives man his wisdom, for when there is no more to learn in books man must turn to nature as his teacher. By studying the truth in nature, the nature of truth will be revealed to him!

KEYWORDS:

Abundance, excess, largeness, freedom, nature, undomesticated large animals, truth, wisdom, man-made law, justice, expansiveness, generosity, happiness, mirth, frivolity, travel, scenery, wealth, rewards, luck, fortune, the higher mind, philosophy, religion, higher learning, hope, optimism, high spiritis, carefree attitudes, ancient civilizations, precious metals, honours, enlightenment, rules the ninth year of anything.

Planetary Hour: Six o'clock

Day of the Week: Thursday
Traverses a Sign: 1 year
Rules: Sagittarius

Saturn

Saturn is the planet of time. It rules the sign Capricorn which starts the winter season. The earth forms a dried crusty cover over itself, delaying the growth processes of nature so that it can replenish for a new season. Underneath this apparent blanket of inactivity vital salts and minerals are slowly forming to bring new substance to all that was taken out of the earth during harvest. The trees are brittle, as the sap (Cancer, which nourished the leaves in Summer) now conserves its strength under a protective coating.

Saturn holds rulership over all that protects and covers. In contrast to the sap in the tree finding its rulership under the Moon (Cancer), the tree bark (or outer protective covering) is ruled by Saturn (Capricorn). The interior of a home is allocated to the Moon, the exterior protective quality of the home is a manifestation of Saturn. The clothes that one wears in order to be protected from the elements reflects the same quality. All that is dry and brittle, coarse and strong is under the rulership of Saturn. All that must be conserved for a duration of time, and all that must be protected is under Saturn's domain. The shell around the nut, the squirrel hoarding his food and the hybernation of animals are typical examples. All that man must conceal to keep for the future; his financial savings, his important beliefs, and the plans that will mature at a later time are part of his Saturnian quality. The wisdom that one has but must delay in using until the proper time or teachable moment presents itself is part of this struggle for preserving that which is most important.

Projects that are slow to mature, the result of painstaking dedication are attributed to Saturn. The shell of the tortoise makes it unable to move about quickly, but neverthless acts as the protection that enables the tortoise to live several hundred years! Saturn strengthens one's character by teaching the value of patience and endurance. Nothing of true worth can exist without Saturn. It binds together all the meaningful pieces that give form to the whole. It helps cement ideas so they can be crystallized into what will one day be accepted as established.

In mythology, this planet has been associated with agriculture, reaping, social order, the establishment of civilization, that which comes through struggle and the mature result of long dedicated effort. As a deity, Saturn was the ruler over the Golden Age of innocence in Rome where order and organization preserved the structure of cultured civilization.

The most powerful function of Saturn is its ability to limit through form that which must not exceed its boundaries. Without form the world would be in chaos. Within the solidified structure of what is, man can conceive a reality that he can deal with. Rules that create guidelines are part of Saturn's domain. Responsibilities, weights and burdens through which man earns his sense of self-worth are part of the limits that Saturn puts on the bargain one makes in order to live within his society. In essence it is the superego force that through its austere quality tells man what will give him the security of the harvest he is seeking and what is off his path.

Spiritually, Saturn rules the path of initiation through which man reaches his greater self by causing him to adhere to specific disciplines which strengthen his character and solidify his being. Through his Saturn placement, he learns perspective and that Karma (the result of past actions) can actually be mastered as one slowly gains control over oneself.

Saturn sometimes gives man a sense of bondage, and by delaying him from reaching his goals helps him to grow more determined, strengthens his faith, and matures his insight concerning values that represent the greatest meaning to him. Saturn is the teacher. It symbolizes the stumbling blocks that man can change into the stepping stones of his evolution.

The ties that bind are under Saturn's rulership; ties between families, ancestors, marriage, friendships, the cementing of objects through various sorts of adhesives, strings, ropes, chains, cables, connectors of various types, the continuity of linear time as seen through watches, clocks, calendars and schedules. Saturn holds that which must be held. It protects that which must be protected. It conserves that which must be conserved,

Ideas, thoughts, and philosophies which are passed on from one generation to the next, maturing through the ages, show the wisdom inherent in Saturn's domain. All that is carefully thought out and planned, all that is modest and tempered with a careful consideration of reality, and all that is goal-oriented is the result of Saturn. The planet speaks of realism as opposed to dreams, truth as opposed to ideals and myths, and that which can be accomplished through sincere effort.

More than any other planet, Saturn teaches man his true worth. In a mundane sense, it gives him his dignity and prestige. In a philosophical sense, it teaches him how to find meaning in life. Its true worth is usually not recognized for centuries. The great books written hundreds and thousands of years ago are even now only partially appreciated in all of the wisdom they contain. The culture preserved from civilizations of the past provides us with foundations upon which we may build the present and future. The wisdom, intelligence and foresight of Saturn extends many centuries into the future. Thus, Saturn's lesson teaches us to dedicate our life to something that will outlast it.

KEYWORDS:

Endurance, dedication, wisdom, time, age, dignity, sobriety, completeness, practicality, virtue, control, per spective, fullness, ability to conserve, insight, firmness in convictions, understanding of traditions, ability to build on ancestry or use wisdom from history, continuity, guided, purposeful, respectful, understands limitations, realibility, dependability, disciplined, constant, devoted, binding, protective, rules the tenth year of anything, sound reason, preservation of culture.

Planetary Hour: Four o'clock
Day of the Week: Saturday
Traverses a Sign: 2½ years
Rules: Capricorn

Uranus

Uranus is the planet of change. It rules the sign Aquarius during the middle of the northern winter season when nature is preparing herself for the future year by releasing the past. The earth is furthest from the Sun at this time and experiences a change in its electrical charge so that the atoms, molecules, minerals, salts, and other elements can rearrange themselves for the freshness of the new season.

Where Saturn symbolized the binding together for preservation of what must be conserved, Uranus symbolizes the release of all that is no longer useful. It holds rulership over the dispersal of energy and the changes that take place between energy and matter. Because of Saturn's winter blanket, most of these changes go unseen. Uranus symbol— izes turbulence within the silence, change within the structure, redirection within the form. And, from these changes comes the breakdown of old forms to make way for the new.

Uranus acts to break established patterns, scatter that which has been bound too tightly, and dissipate all that is no longer useful. It hints of future progress, and gives man glimpses of what is not accepted now but will one day be a part of established society. Looking at all that is rigidly structured in the world, Uranus asks the question, "why?," and from its answers seeks to discover new and better pathways that symbolize inventive improvement for the human race.

Electricity, television and radio waves, gadgets, inventions, unique patterns, radar and sonar, and all that is scientific and science-fiction are under the rulership of Uranus. Jules Verne, the author of *Twenty Thousand Leagues Under the Sea* was influenced by Uranian energy.

Man's humane concern for his fellow man is a Uranian concept. Doing not for oneself, but for the advancement and progress of one's race is symbolic of the winter season which sacrifices itself for the coming seeds of spring.

Up through Saturn, man strives to create his life, build his foundations, and understand his purpose. He sees himself as living in a person-centered world. Uranus, however, brings man to a different awareness for it shows him how much he is a product of the universal forces. He comes to realize that he does not control his world; that he is an impersonal part of nature receiving and expressing ideas from the creative cosmic flow. Much like the tree that grows more in the rainy season and less when the weather is dry, he is part of nature's plan. His will is part of the Divine will. His ideas are part of the Divine idea. His inspirations are part of nature's inspiration.

The entire winter season symbolizes "surrender" as the earth rests and changes in preparation for its activities in the future. Uranus symbolizes the surrender of the personal will to the greater cosmic energy. Planning is replaced with nature's spontaneity. Continuity is replaced with the ever-changing now, that is never the same as it was a moment ago.

Uranus heightens the intellect, stimulates interest, increases awareness and attracts one to all things that are new and different. The mental activity of this planet inspires us to ask questions, and from these questions, we grow. Man becomes aware that the world contains differences. He begins to understand and appreciate these differences rather than seeking sameness. Thus, he opens his mind to new ideas, new philosophies and new developments. Nature has rules (Saturn) but nature also breaks her own rules (Uranus) to develop new ones. The rules of nature describe the ordinary, that which is expected because of repeated occurence. Uranus represents all that is possible through what appears to us to be "chance occurrence." Yet, the entire concept of "chance" is also a law of nature.

The Guiness World Book of Records and *Ripley's Believe it or Not*, describe the chance occurrences in nature, showing the Uranian quality of uniqueness. Science, which seeks to discover and categorize nature is a product of Uranus. To "discover" is to find that which is unique and somehow different from what is already known. But, for man to find the uniqueness in himself and his environment he must be free.

Uranus frees the intellect from the shackles of overcumbersome burdens of tradition. It helps one to think in new and original pathways which will ultimately lead mankind to discover all that is not yet known.

URANUS KEYWORDS:

Enlightenment, individuality, eccentricity, discovery, research, originality, uniqueness, awareness, heightens the intellect, tradition-breaking, fair-mindedness, freedom, intellectual development, the will of nature, the impersonal self, unbinding, advancement, progress, selflessness, science, science-fiction, understanding, futuristic, cleverness, rules the eleventh year of anything, change, electricity, exploration, man's humanity to man, crusading for the underdog.

Planetary Hour: Not yet established
Day of the Week: Wednesday
Traverses a Sign: 7 years
Rules: Aquarius

Neptune

Neptune is the planet of fluids. It rules the sign Pisces as the end of the year dissolves away, sacrificing itself for the new season in the northern hemisphere. We see the winter snows melt. The earth softens, and nature shows her yielding quality as she surrenders her coldness to the coming warmth of spring.

Neptune holds rulership over all that loosens. Vague impressions not clearly definable in words, liquid streams of thought that bring out the romantic instinct, dreams which free the unconscious, the fantasy-like quality of the imagination, and man's intuitive feel for his environment are all characteristic of Neptune.

As the higher octave of Venus, Neptune expands the love nature, soothing and softening man's relationship with his environment. It dissolves his desire to fight and replaces it with an unconscious understanding of his place in the universe. Through this he is able to experience a oneness with his surroundings, and instead of misunderstanding the ways of nature he is able to blend and flow with it. From this he develops compassion for the world he lives in.

The period of impressionism in music and the arts is symbolic of Neptune, as the planet concerns all that approaches the abstract part of nature that is barely discernable, yet unmistakably there. Subtle nuances, vague hints, mysteries that present intrigue and the intangible attractions in life that draw one from one question to another are Neptunian.

Many things come from the liquid state and thus originate from Neptune. Glass, mirrors (that create illusions), plastics, paints, oils, films (which must be developed in liquid) and all that is smooth and flowing are in Neptune's realm. Tears, sorrow, deep feelings, intuition, and unspoken communication that flows between people are manifestations of Neptune.

The planet rules the subtle part of the unconscious; those thoughts that are slightly below the threshold of conscious awareness, but from time to time rise like the crest of a wave to the conscious level. An individual's taste in terms of his selection of foods, colors, textures, come from this level of the unconscious. Subliminal advertising is directed towards Neptunian perception.

Meditative states of awareness that lull the mind or body into a state of relaxation, hypnosis, intangible beliefs, doubts, vague disillusions, confusion, and the process of forgetting, or losing thoughts and ideas are all part of the loosening action of Neptune as it dissolves the past. In higher states of consciousness, man understands that "The softest thing in the universe overcomes the hardest thing in the universe."* Neptune unquestionably symbolizes the softest things in the universe. Its ever- pouring nature keeps filling man with the pure essence of Divine love. When an individual is able to tap this "essence" he consciously loosens his defenses for he realizes that much of what his mind is fighting is nothing more than illusions created in his subtle unconscious. Neptune gives the opportunity to rise above these illusions through creative inspiration; artistically, musically, or aesthetically as it invites man to open his heart to a higher music which comes from his Soul.

Neptune is a planet of depth. Much of the knowledge of mysticism comes from probing through the illusions and misconceptions of reality that mankind has accepted. The great mysteries of life are concealed in the subtle reality of Neptune rather than the gross reality that man deals with in his mundane levels. Yet, because of the planet's fluid effect, unconscious understandings gained through intuition and impression often seep through to conscious levels when one is least aware of it. The act of making love often brings one to experience contact with Neptune's subtle music.

——

*Tao Te Ching, Lao Tsu, translated by Gia-Fu Feng and Jane English, published by Random House, New York, 1972 (FORTY-THREE)

Those under the rulership of this planet experience gentleness, kindness, a giving compassionate nature, and a oneness with the universe they live in. They can feel how Neptune constantly gives and gives selflessly pouring her waters of Divine love for all who need. The holy ceremony of baptism is the symbolic acting out of Neptune's blessings. Christ himself, was a symbol of Neptunian love when he gave of himself in the Piscean age.

This giving nature is such that it does not ask for anything in return. "Jainism" as practiced by Mahatma Gandhi says that all one can do (whether he consciously knows it or not) is give. And, the more he is willing to give, the more he is supplied from the infinite source. Neptune touches the infinite in man's understanding. Unlike the Saturnian borders and boundaries and the often hectic changes of Uranus, Neptune smoothly expands one's consciousness so that out of the inner aloneness that every individual feels, he has the opportunity to realize a blending oneness with everything and everyone. When an individual can do this, he knows he has touched the essence of Neptune's truth.

Neptune has never been seen as a planet of wisdom, but all of the outer planets possess a certain essence of wisdom—each different than the other. Neptune's wisdom comes from man being able to tap into the creative flow of infinite wisdom that always existed and always will. Effortlessly, it is possible to know what should be known and forget what is unnecessary to remember. Neptune is the mind of nature in its highest octave.

KEYWORDS:

Dissolving, softening, sacrificial, compassionate, gentle, fluid, liquids, drugs, illusions, confusion, the subtle unconscious, dreams, meditation, hypnosis, loosening, pure essence, flowing, artistic, creative, inspirational, visionary, idealistic, imaginative, rules all that is formless, subtlety, impressions, fantasy, mystery, intrigue, psychic, intuitive, generous, blending, the Christ Consciousness, rules the twelfth year of anything, Divine love.

Planetary Hour: Not established
Day of the Week: Friday
Traverses a Sign: 14 years
Rules: Pisces

Pluto

Pluto is the last of the known planets to be discovered. It holds co-rulership with Mars over the sign Scorpio, symbolizing the release of the harvest, the end of the northern growing season.

It represents the unknown, all that is hidden from view, the deepest mysteries of life, and the core of life energy itself through the unconscious universal drive to reproduce the species. Anything that comes from the earth is ruled by Pluto. Diamonds and precious metals which are mined from the earth, the wealth that the earth yields in all forms are under Pluto's domain.

Neptune holds rulership over the subtle unconscious, and Pluto rules the raw unconscious at the very roots of man's Soul. It is the planet that causes upheaval, bringing to the surface all that must be eliminated in the process of regeneration. Thus, it is often seen as a destructive force, for it can symbolize the shadow in man's life, or the darker side that likes to destroy as much as the lighter side likes to create. One cannot know light without darkness. If man is good then he is also bad. If he is constructive, he is also capable of uprooting his constructiveness. If he is a blessing, then he is also a curse. These are yin and yang levels that balance each other when man's higher nature is brought to light.

The hidden wisdom that Pluto surfaces enables an individual to be decisive about the conclusions he reaches, knowing that what he knows is correct. Pluto is also the planet of power. An individual gains power or control over himself when he stops lingering in decisions he has already made and asserts himself on all levels. The power to transform one's being and make complete changes in one's lifestyle comes from Pluto.

The undeniable fact that man is a mortal being is a Plutonic truth, and we learn how to accept chapters that close in life, never again to be re-opened, as Pluto energy makes us ready for new experiences. Graduation from school, moving from one location to another, the end of a relationship or marriage, the selling of a long-held possession are all manifestations of how Pluto can close doors behind us so that we can regenerate and change our lives.

Sharing the rulership of Scorpio with Mars, Pluto holds rulership over the unconscious sexual drive. Where Mars indicates how an individual expresses sexuality, Pluto recognizes that sexuality is a universal force in nature. Stemming from the unseen quarries of earth, (the division between conscious and unconscious mind states) Pluto is the primal mover of mankind. Unlike the other planets which exert their force on the earth, Pluto's force reaches within the earth. Pluto's orbit forms the outer boundary of our solar system, and contains all life within the energies of all the planets in our solar system. We cannot transform or transcend the nature of these energies without confronting Pluto, mythologically called the God of the underworld.

Pluto rules criminals, violation of moral standards, upheaval of past structures, man's baser nature, subversion, lust, uprooting, volcanoes, earthquakes, geysers, natural disasters, policemen, wars, atomic power, and destruction of all kinds. It also holds influence over mass movements that create sweeping changes in man's evolution. Politically destructive movements which incorporate the use of force, violence, and the infiltration of free minds are Plutonian in nature.

All these characteristics, however, are only one side of the power of Pluto. Destructiveness, endings, and upheaval have very positive qualities. The science of medicine seeks to find endings to disease and is ruled by Pluto. The destruction of decayed buildings for the purpose of building new ones in their place is a positive manifestation of this energy. Reaching deep into the bowels of the earth for the darkest of minerals (coal) is the way we find diamonds.

To understand the true nature of Pluto we must realize that things are rarely as they seem. Light is only needed where there is darkness. Pluto is a planet of both. Fossils, excavations, the entire science of archaeology, the discovery of ancient relics, the deciphering of hieroglyphics, and the uncovering of great mysteries are all in Pluto's domain. The forces of darkness, whether based on superstition or reality, depend largely upon the Plutonic beliefs of the unconscious.

Shipwrecks lost at sea, the Bermuda triangle, the lost city of Atlantis, the civilization of Lemuria, and the secrets within the Egyptian pyramids are under the rulership of Pluto. Whatever is hidden from view whether it be in physical enclosures such as mines, caves, cellars, closets, or enclosures in consciousness, concealing the secret unknown quantities of life, Pluto rules all that must be brought to the surface to be understood and then transformed. It is only when man explores all that he does not know, that he is able to discover the things and ideas through which he can regenerate.

KEYWORDS:
Unconscious, hidden, secrets, the unknown, endings, destructiveness, upheaval, evolution, archaeology, riches mined from the earth, depth, power, the darker side of life, transformations, research, medicine, great wisdom, insight, rules the eighth year of anything, fossils, excavations, heiroglyphics, codes, unconscious memories, the masses, sex, death and regeneration, rebirth, finding that which was lost.

Planetary Hour: not established
Day of the week: not established
Traverses a Sign: 20 years
Co-rules: Scorpio

The Planetary Octaves

Each of the inner planets (or personal planets) is related to an outer planet whose impersonal vibration tends to amplify and bring out the finer qualities of the inner planet.

INNER PLANET	MERCURY	VENUS	MARS
Idealized in the qualities of the OUTER PLANET	URANUS	NEPTUNE	PLUTO

Mercury rules the intellect. Uranus is the planet of genius, heightening and stimulating the thought processes towards discovery, originality, and uniqueness. Venus rules personal love. Neptune is the planet of Divine love, and adds a more cosmic flow to the love instinct. Mars is the planet of activity and the outward expression of the sex drive. Pluto symbolizes the energy needed for the regeneration or reproduction of the species.

The Sun and the Moon stand by themselves as the two luminaries. Jupiter and Saturn act as the energies that balance each other, creating wisdom, understanding and purpose. They symbolize the achievement of centering through expansion and contraction, freedom and confinement, movement and restriction, impatience and delay, overt and covert, spontaneity and thoughtfulness, wealth and poverty, in essence, the yin and yang of creation on all levels.

Thus, we can see that each planet has a purpose which in some way helps to explain another planet. When we understand the nature of all the planets we are able to perceive man's essential role and purpose, within the framework of the forces that are always acting on him.

The Mystical Cycle of the Signs

*T*he twelve signs of the zodiac from Aries to Pisces contain all the expressions of man's planetary energies. Each sign has specific qualities and properties which put it in harmony with nature's plan, and the order that the signs follow is not accidental, but rather shows a sequence of philosophical development starting from a primitive conception of reality and ending with a Divine understanding of man's cosmic nature.

We find the signs Aries, Taurus and Gemini ruled by Mars, Venus and Mercury. These three ruling planets appear to be moving in the direction of the Sun in the natural zodiac. The Sun is the "light" which creates life. The result of Spring is a physical birth in Cancer under the rulership of the Moon. Together these four signs symbolize the first part of man's experience—*his creation.*

The next three signs, Leo, Virgo and Libra, under the rulership of the Sun, Mercury, and Venus show a different picture as the ruling planets move in the direction away from the Sun. These three signs represent what man does for himself with what he is given. The result is found in the sign Scorpio as man interprets his gifts through the use of power, sex, and the ultimate upheaval brought about through his desire nature. Thus, these four signs symbolize the second part of man's experience—*his destruction.*

The next three signs, Sagittarius, Capricorn, and Aquarius under the rulership of Jupiter, Saturn and Uranus show the three rulers moving still further away from the Sun. Through these signs, man reaches his higher cosmic understanding of his place in the universe, culminating in the last sign of the zodiac, Pisces, where he begins to understand the nature of divine love. These four signs symbolize the third part of man's experience—*his redemption* and realization of his cosmic being.

The first three signs lead to Cancer under the rulership of the Moon, which symbolizes the *birth of the body.* The next three signs lead to Scorpio under the rulership of Mars and Pluto, symbolizing the *use of the body.* The final three signs lead to Pisces under the rulership of Neptune which

ZODIAC SIGN	RULING PLANET	PURPOSE	CYCLE
ARIES	Mars	Seed	
TAURUS	Venus	Egg	BIRTH
GEMINI	Mercury	Mitosis	CREATION
CANCER	MOON	Birth	
LEO	Sun	Free Will	
VIRGO	Mercury	Order	USE
LIBRA	Venus	Balance	DESTRUCTION
SCORPIO	PLUTO	Discontent Upheaval	
SAGITTARIUS	Jupiter	Truth	
CAPRICORN	Saturn	Redemption	SURRENDER
AQUARIUS	Uranus	Selflessness	REDEMPTION
PISCES	NEPTUNE	Divine love	

The Signs of the Zodiac

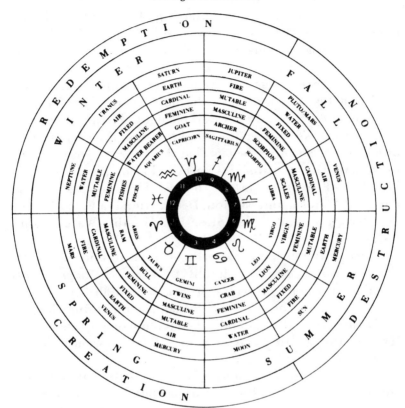

symbolizes the *absolution of the body*. We can see how the twelve signs of the zodiac work together as a symbol of the complete plan for existence. It is not coincidental that each of the cycles ends under the rulership of a psychic feminine planet, for the three stages of man become fulfilled only when he recognizes his receptivity to the universe he lives in.

These three cycles of man—his creation, his destruction, and his redemption—culminate in the signs Cancer, Scorpio and Pisces, the water element. If this were not enough to make the seeking mind question the very essence of life itself, consider the fact that these three signs in order represent the Cardinal (Cancer), Fixed (Scorpio) and Mutable (Pisces) modes of being. Thus, creation is a Cardinal-Water manifestation; Destruction is a Fixed-Water manifestation, and Redemption is a Mutable-Water manifestation.

One of the deepest mysteries of life is to know *when to let the water run* (cardinality), *when to turn it off* (fixedness), and *when to alter its course* (mutability). Water symbolizes emotion. When allowed to run, things begin; when turned off, things end; when its course is altered, man realizes the greatest mystery of all—the essence of his *control!*

The three cycles all ending in water signs show another purpose to the plan of life. Nature needs the cohesiveness of water to bind things together (Cancer), the turbulence of water to tear things apart (Scorpio), and the smooth clearness of water (Pisces) to purify. It is only when man's emotions (Cancer) are transformed through Scorpio that he can become in touch with a higher form of emotion (Pisces) that is in tune with cosmic love. This perception helps us understand what Jesus meant when he said, "I will pit son against sire, mother against daughter, and stir up the murky waters, and then only will you know peace." He was really confronting the emotions of family (Cancer), in order to disturb the cemented distortions (Scorpio), so that people could see a clearer stream of consciousness (Pisces) to swim in! In more modern times, the singer, Donovan, in *Essence to Essence*, mystically describes this same water trinity through the words "First there is a river (Cancer), then there isn't (Scorpio), then there is (Pisces)!"

The Decanates

*O*ne of the most fascinating areas in astrology comes from the subdivision of zodiac signs into *decanates*. Each sign of thirty degrees contains three ten degree decanates. These subdivisions bring the full meaning of each sign into clear focus.

The first decanate of any sign is under the rulership of the planet that rules the full sign. Thus, the first 10 degrees of Aries is under the rulership of Mars, while the first 10 degrees of Taurus is under the rulership of Venus. The second decanate of a sign is ruled by the planet that rules the next sign of the same element. Thus, to find the ruler of the second decanate of Aries, we have to first realize that Aries is a Fire sign. The next sign in the Fire element is Leo, whose ruler is the Sun. The second decanate of Aries then, is the Leo part of Aries and therefore is under the rulership of the Sun. The third or final decanate of Aries is ruled by the planet that rules the fire sign after Leo. This brings us to Sagittarius, whose ruler is Jupiter. The final decanate of Aries, then, is the Sagittarius part of Aries and falls under Jupiter's rulership.

If we want to see the three decanates of Taurus and their rulers, we have only to look at the three Earth element signs, beginning with Taurus. Thus, the first decanate is the Taurus part of Taurus, under the rulership of Venus. The second decanate comes from the succeeding Earth sign, Virgo, and is under the rulership of Mercury. The final decanate comes from the last Earth sign, Capricorn, and is under the rulership of Saturn.

The first decanate of any sign is always ruled by the sign itself, with the second and third decanates always following its same element in succession. Thus, the first decanate of Aquarius (Air element) does not begin with the first air sign Gemini, but with Aquarius itself. Then Gemini, the next air sign followed by Libra (the air sign after Gemini) completes the three decanates of Aquarius

It becomes apparent from this system that different parts of a sign exhibit different characteristics. While each zodiac sign has its own ruling planet, the three decanates within it have a personal planet which holds influence over the manifestations of that part of the sign. Thus, an individual born with Venus in Pisces will not experience the love emotion (Venus) in the same way as another individual born with Venus in Pisces within a different decanate of the sign. If Venus appears at the fifth degree of Pisces (Neptune-ruled and Neptune decanate) the person is usually considered gentle, sensitive and compassionate. With Neptune being the higher octave of Venus, it is almost akin to the love of a monk or nun, sincerely giving in silent ways without asking in return. But, consider Venus in Pisces appearing at the twenty eighth or twenty ninth degree of the sign. Here in the third decanate, Venus is still under the Neptune rulership of Pisces, but it appears in the Scorpio part of the sign. Thus, on personal levels, the love emotion (Venus) is influenced by the co-rulers of Scorpio; Mars and Pluto. The intense sexual drive of these two planets changes what one would expect of the Venus in Pisces placement. Consider also that planets on the cusp (within three degrees of a sign change) also receive some influence from the next sign. This late degree Venus in Pisces is close enough to

Aries to be feeling a still further Mars influence from its rulership in Aries. Thus, the fifth degree Venus in Pisces has the flavor of Neptune-Neptune, while the twenty eighth or twenty ninth degree Venus in Pisces has the flavor of Neptune, Pluto-Mars, Mars! Unquestionably, the two will act very differently as the planetary energies are expressed through lifestyle and experiences.

The decanates work on two different levels. At first, they seem to be paradoxical, but they symbolize different things. The first decanate of any sign is somewhat primitive, subjective, and thirsting for experience. The double rulership is in agreement between the planet that rules the sign and the planet that rules the decanate and causes a harmonious energy pattern. The second decanate, however, brings into play the next sign of the same element and its ruling planet. Thus, the individual experiences two forces. Whenever two forces are felt, there is always yin and yang, decision-making, crises, and some amount of turbulence. The lifestyle of the second decanate of any sign becomes more hectic for the individual than if he were experiencing the lifestyle of the first decanate. The third decanate represents a rather unique experience. Under the rulership of the planet that rules the sign itself, it is at the same time experiencing some of what the first decanate experiences, but it also concerns itself with the objective endings of the sign. Thus, the third decanate is both subjective (first decanate) and objective (third decanate) at the same time. The third decanate has the ability to make mature and clear decisions, can see the vast scope of things without having to go through the arena of experience (so common to the second decanate), and is often unwilling to go through "wrong" experiences that the second decanate sees as the only way one can learn about life!

Consider decanates analogous to the three cycles of human experience that develop through the signs. The first cycle resulted in Cancer (the Moon) and symbolized birth. The second cycle resulted in Scorpio (Mars and Pluto) and symbolized use. And the third cycle resulted in Pisces (Neptune) and symbolized absolution. The decanates work in much the same manner. The primitive qualities of the first decanate symbolize the need to experience which results in birth. The crises experiences of the second decanate symbolize use. The wisdom and maturity of the third decanate come from absolution and the ability to surrender to the forces that be.

Visualize three individuals each having their Sun in Aquarius but at five degrees, fifteen degrees, and twenty five dgrees respectively. Aquarius is the sign of unique ideas, and for the sake of argument, consider that these three individuals are inventors. During the course of the year as the Sun will pass through Aquarius, it will activate the fifth degree of Aquarius first. Ten days later it will be approximately at the fifteenth degree. And still ten days later it will reach the twenty-fifth degree of the sign. The inventor having his Sun at the fifth degree of Aquarius will unquestionably be the first of the three to have a particular idea, but in its birth through the first decanate, the idea may be premature. Approximately ten days later, the second inventor comes up with the same idea. This time, however, the idea is somewhat more cultivated and through the yin and yang decision-making processes that go on in the second decanate the individual is able to consider the practicality of this idea. When the idea strikes the person who has the Sun in the third decanate of Aquarius, he knows instantly the essence of its worth. Through his unconscious knowledge that he is not the first to receive the idea, he does not have to make hasty decisions on it. Thus, he can weigh the cosmic value of its lasting worth before he acts. Thus, we see how the concept of birth, use, and surrender to natural cosmic law work through the three decanates of a sign.

On another level, which may seem paradoxical, we must confront the differences between how the decanates appear in early and late signs in the zodiac. Any one of the signs of

the Spring season will have three decanates which consecutively evolve its element through the year. Any one of the
later signs in the year (particularly those in the Winter
season) will have three decanates which consecutively
"devolve" the element of the sign. In diagram A, notice how
in each of the Spring signs, the decanates move in the
direction of fulfilling the year.

SPRING SEASON								
ARIES			*TAURUS*			*GEMINI*		
ruled by Mars			ruled by Venus			ruled by Mercury		
First Decan.	*Second Decan.*	*Third Decan.*	*First Decan.*	*Second Decan.*	*Third Decan.*	*First Decan.*	*Second Decan.*	*Third Decan.*
Aries	Leo	Sagittarius	Taurus	Virgo	Capricorn	Gemini	Libra	Aquarius
ruled by Mars	ruled by Sun	ruled by Jupiter	ruled by Venus	ruled by Mercury	ruled by Saturn	ruled by Mercury	ruled by Venus	ruled by Uranus

Diagram A.

Aries, Leo, and Sagittarius follow in direct order.
Taurus, Virgo and Capricorn also follow in this order. So do
Gemini, Libra and Aquarius. Thus, in each of these three
Spring season signs, the decanates show a progression
towards a higher or more fulfilled evolution. In each case,
the third decanate is under the cosmic rulership of an outer

planet. There is some consistency between the development of a sign through its decanates and the concept that a sign moves from birth at 0 degrees to full maturity at 30 degrees. The seeming paradox to this occurs when we consider the latter signs of the zodiac. Diagram B shows the signs of the winter season, their decanates and rulers.

Notice that each sign ends under the decanate influence of an inner personal planet. Thus, the progressive evolution through a sign does not appear to work as it did in the spring signs (Aries, Taurus, Gemini).

What really occurs is that each sign progresses towards its last decanate ruler. Thus, in the early signs of the zodiac, we see how lower mind states progress to more universal attitudes as we move through each sign. In the latter signs,

Diagram B.

WINTER SEASON

CAPRICORN ruled by Saturn			AQUARIUS ruled by Uranus			PISCES ruled by Neptune		
First Decan.	*Second Decan.*	*Third Decan.*	*First Decan.*	*Second Decan.*	*Third Decan.*	*First Decan.*	*Second Decan.*	*Third Decan.*
Capricorn	Taurus	Virgo	Aquarius	Gemini	Libra	Pisces	Cancer	Scorpio
ruled by	ruled by	ruled by	ruled by	ruled by	ruled by	ruled by	ruled by	ruled by
Saturn	Venus	Mercury	Uranus	Mercury	Venus	Neptune	Moon	Pluto/ Mars

however, the third decanate (which contains the culmination of wisdom of the sign) is always ruled by a personal planet. This lead us to a very interesting observation. The early signs of the zodiac start in primitive instincts, or lower-mind personal viewpoints. The lessons in these signs is how one realizes higher states of consciousness by realizing the objective goals of the last decanate ruler. In the latter signs, objective consciousness is the starting point, and the individual must learn how to use the raw material of the sign in his everyday mundane life (as these signs) begin with universal intelligence and progress towards mundane activity in their last decanate).

What is extremely interesting is that the decanate progression from inner planet rulerships towards outer planet rulerships stays pure only during the first four signs of the zodiac, (Aries, Taurus, Gemini, Cancer) during man's Birth Cycle. In these signs, the individual struggles to achieve his higher self.

In the middle signs (Leo, Virgo, Libra and Scorpio) the first decanate always feels the influence of an inner planet. The universal outer planetary rulership is reached in the second decanate and progresses towards an inner planet rulership in the last decanate. Scorpio (under the rulership of Pluto and Mars) has the influence of both an outer and an inner planet in its first decanate, but, because Pluto symbolizes the volatile upheaval through which lower emotion becomes transformed, it is again only through the second decanate rulership (Pisces, ruled by Neptune) that a higher stream of universal emotion starts to manifest. Thus, each of these four signs feels its source through personal levels, reaches universal understanding in the second decanate (through strife) and again returns to a personal level in the last decanate as the ultimate goal of the sign. Unlike the Birth Cycle where an outer planet (signifying what has already been transformed from personal to cosmic levels) shows the raw material of the sign (through its first decanate rulership)* these signs understand through experience that a higher reality is possible, but it is extremely difficult for the individual to feel in touch with it as a natural source of his existence. Thus, he can point it out to others, perhaps even see all the flaws in mankind, but he does not understand it for himself. This manifests as the Destruction Cycle (these middle four signs of the zodiac) as man struggles with his ego, trying to correct the problems of mankind through himself rather than identifying with the universal source.

In the last four signs (Sagittarius, Capricorn, Aquarius and Pisces) the Redemption Cycle manifests as the individual drawing on a cosmic source (the raw material of the sign, under the first decanate rulership of an outer planet), learns how man can solve every-day problems (the inner planet goal of the last decanate) by keeping in touch with universal truths.

In the process of chart interpretation it is important to consider the decanate in which each planet falls (as we saw through our earlier Venus in Pisces example), as well as looking at the overall picture of which decanates have more emphasis and which planetary rulerships are either outstanding or absent. When we do this, the specific nature of a particular decanate can be considered in relation to a planet as well as in terms of the evolution of the sign.

In the horoscope of Carl Sandburg, we find:

First decanate planets	2
Second decanate planets	5
Third decanate planets	3

---

*Pluto (as the co-ruler of the first decanate of Scorpio) signifies the on-going transformations, or the process of change itself, but not the ability to apply what has already been transformed.

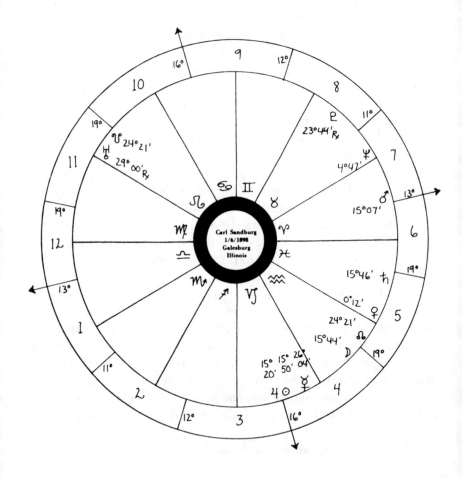

Birth data obtained from "An Astrological Who's Who" by Marc Penfield. Arcane Books, York Harbor, Maine, 1972, p. 417.

CARL SANDBURG

Decanate Rulers		Sign Rulers	Total Rulers	
Sun:	1	1	Sun:	2
Moon:	1	0	Moon:	1
Mercury:	2	0	Mercury:	2
Venus:	3	2	Venus:	5
Mars:	1	1	Mars:	2
Jupiter:	0	0	Jupiter:	0
Saturn:	1	3	Saturn:	4
Uranus:	0	1	Uranus:	1
Neptune:	1	2	Neptune:	3
Pluto:	0	0	Pluto:	0

The emphasis on second decanate planets shows a great deal of concern with yin and yang qualities, comparisons, and the dual nature of existence. His Sun in Capricorn falls in the second decanate of a Redemption sign. Thus, he would have experienced the essence of struggle through which mankind seeks redeeming qualities. His poetry and writings reflect the truth and beauty that man aspires to reach amidst the conflict that is forever a torment to his soul. When we determine the number of decanate and sign rulers we see a predominance of Venus and Saturn, the two planets which symbolize a concern with the crystillization of aesthetic beauty and inner depth.

In the horoscope of Kahlil Gibran, one of history's great men of wisdom and words, we find:

First decanate planets:	2
Second decanate planets:	4
Third decanate planets:	4

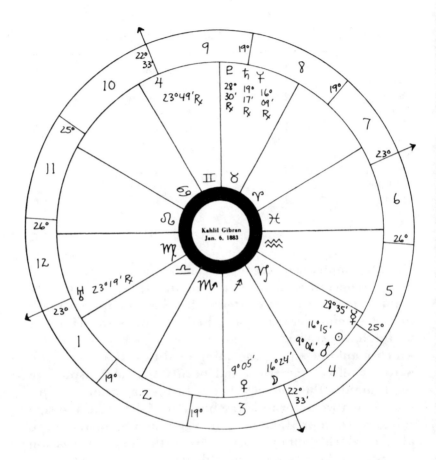

Birth data obtained from "An Astrological Who's Who" by Marc Penfield. Arcane Books, York Harbor, Maine, 1972, p. 185

KAHIL GILBRAN

Decanate Rulers			Sign Rulers	Total Rulers	
Sun:	0	0	Sun:	0	
Moon:	0	0	Moon:	0	
Mercury:	3	2	Mercury:	5	
Venus:	2	3	Venus:	5	
Mars:	1	0	Mars:	1	
Jupiter:	1	2	Jupiter:	3	
Saturn:	2	3	Saturn:	5	
Uranus:	1	0	Uranus:	1	
Neptune:	0	0	Neptune:	0	
Pluto:	0	0	Pluto:	0	

Mercury, Venus and Saturn are the three planets which flavor the rest of the horoscope. It is interesting to note how much of Gibran's poetry speaks about youth (Mercury), love (Venus) and age (Saturn).

The emphasis of energy is centered in the second and third decanates, indicating a concern for dealing with the opposing conflicts of life, along with a cosmic understanding of why they should exist. It is interesting to note that in both Carl Sandburg's and Kahlil Gibran's chart, two men of great knowledge, with a deep understanding of nature, there is little emphasis on the so-called primitive qualities of the first decanate.

Frank Lloyd Wright, the architect, shows a different combination of decanate rulership:

First decanate planets:	4
Second decanate planets:	5
Third decanate planets:	1

Where Sandburg and Gibran were great thinkers, Wright was more of a "doer." His creative need, though beautiful and unique, was nevertheless expressed on a more primitive level. He built homes that cooperated with the environment, shaping his forms to fit the forms of nature.

The cosmic maturity that we find in Sandburg and Gibran (second and third decanate emphasis) is replaced in Wright with initiatory flamboyance which marked the pioneering instinct rather than the music of a poet!

FRANK LLOYD WRIGHT

Decanate Rulers		Sign Rulers	Total Rulers	
Sun:	1	0	Sun:	1
Moon:	1	2	Moon:	3
Mercury:	3	4	Mercury:	7
Venus:	2	2	Venus:	4
Mars:	2	1	Mars:	3
Jupiter:	0	1	Jupiter:	1
Saturn:	0	0	Saturn:	0
Uranus:	1	0	Uranus:	1
Neptune:	0	0	Neptune	0
Pluto:	1	0	Pluto:	1

Notice the strong predominance of Mercury holding seven total rulerships. We would expect to find Mercurial energy, which influences perception, mathematics, the understanding of spatial realationships, strongly accented in the chart of a successful architect. Interestingly enough, he is a Gemini, the sign ruled by Mercury. Notice the absence of Saturn decanates, a quality we might expect to find in the chart of an architect. Frank LLoyd Wright was not as much a builder of form (Saturn) as he was able to understand the relationship between form and beauty in nature. This is clearly a Mercury/Venus influence as his decanates indicate.

To understand these three charts on a deeper level, we can explore the evolutionary qualities of the Sun signs in terms of the decanates. Carl Sandburg's Sun appears in the second decanate of Capricorn, or the Taurus (Venus-ruled) part of the sign. Capricorn's three decanates are: Capricorn,

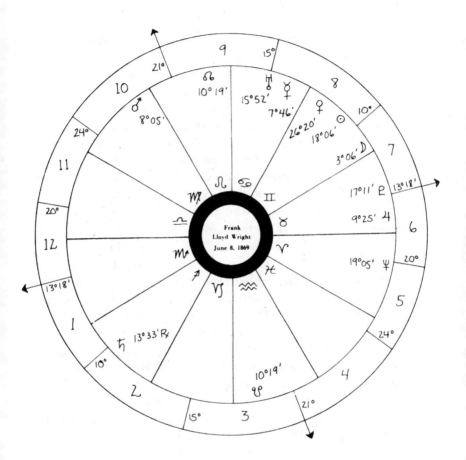

Birth data obtained from "An Astrological Who's Who" by Marc Penfield. Arcane Books, York Harbor, Maine, 1972, p. 498

Taurus, and Virgo under the respective rulerships of Saturn, Venus and Mercury. Capricorn progresses from the first decanate, the concept of conservation (Saturn) to the second decanate, the love of what is protected and secured (Venus), to the third decanate, the understanding of finite order in the universe (Mercury). With his second decanate Sun, Sandburg's works would have concerned themselves with a deep Capricornian appreciation of the natural qualities of conservation. The emphasis on the second decanate combines a strong desire to preserve (Capricorn) the natural beauty (Venus) of a season from the past (Saturn). Kahlil Gibran also had the Sun in the second decanate of Capricorn, and we find a similar thinker. Both men were poets (Venus) who tried to preserve (Capricorn) the wisdom (Saturn) of the ages.

Frank Lloyd Wright had the Sun in the second decanate of Gemini. Under the rulership of Venus (the Libra part of Gemini) we see a concern for aesthetic qualities, but Venus is acting in combination with Mercury rather than Saturn. Thus, Wright created architectural innovation, but has not been remembered in the same way as Sandburg or Gibran. The sign, Gemini moves through its three decanates under the rulerships of Mercury (Gemini), Venus (Libra), and Uranus (Aquarius) showing mental evolution that progresses from an understanding of duality to an understanding of aesthetic harmony and finally culminating in the higher mental qualities which can sometimes manifest as pure genius. Wright's Sun symbolizes the middle of this evolutionary ladder symbolizing how one's life can manifest through the understanding of aesthetic harmony.

Interestingly enough, all three men are second decanate Suns, showing that they all confronted crises, knew about duality, and stuggled through much conflict in order to make their contributions to the world.

It is important to understand how to use decanates in this manner as well as applying them to all planets in the chart, so that the individual under consideration can be seen in full perspective. In this way the potential for development, unfoldment, or evolution shows a cosmic pattern and purpose to the lifestyle.

The Duads

A great paradox exists in man's conception of his individuality. It is of course true that each person is unique, but he is at the same time similar to all other people. If we look at nature, every tree, bush and plant exhibits its own unique properties, yet they share much in common. They all have roots, stems, branches and leaves; they all depend upon the same elements for survival even though they may be of different species.

Man has a tendency to categorize competitively: he sees qualities as "better than," or "worse than." He sees the capabilities and opportunities of different zodiac signs this same way. Philosophically, we know that we are a combination of all the signs.

The Duads show this even more than the timed chart. Where the decanates create three equal 10 degree subdivisions of a sign, the duads go still further. They separate the 30 degrees of a sign into twelve equal parts of 2½ degrees each. Each segment represents one of the twelve signs of the zodiac. The potential for experiencing the entire zodiac then, is contained within each sign.

Like the decanates, the duads in each sign start with the same rulership as the sign itself. Thus, the first duad or 2½ degrees of Aries is the Aries (Mars) duad. The second duad is Taurus. The third duad is Gemini, etc., running through the twelve signs to complete the 30 degrees of Aries. The first duad of Taurus, however, will not begin with the beginning of the zodiac, but will start instead with Taurus (the sign itself). The second duad is Gemini, the third Duad is Cancer, etc., running consecutively through all of the signs until the 30 degrees of Taurus is completed. The 360 degree zodiac is divided into twelve equal signs, each of which is further divided into three 10 degree decanates, and twelve 2½ degree duads. If we look for insight into any particular degree of the zodiac, we have a Sign ruler, a Decanate ruler, and a Duad ruler to help us. Together, the three symbolize the complete triad or chord whose resultant sound is really none of the three, but rather how they blend together as one.

From the diagram of signs, decanates and duads we are able to refine our understanding of the zodiac. An individual who has the Sun at twelve degrees of Aries will experience the sign rulership of Aries (Mars), the decanate rulership of Leo (Sun), and the duad rulership of Leo (Sun). Thus, the chord or triad which describes the self expression is a blend of Mars-Sun-Sun; obviously extroverted, powerful and possessing strong qualities of leadership and command. An individual with the Sun at 12½ degress of Aries, however, would experience the Virgo (Mercury-ruled) duad. Even though the Sun signs are the same, and the decanate remains unchanged, the blend of three rulers is now different. The resulting Mars-Sun-Mercury is more active, more mentally inclined, and somewhat less powerful than the combination of Mars-Sun-Sun. From this example, it becomes easy to see how individuals born even a day or two apart can be quite different.

The entire system of Duads is extremely revealing. A study of the diagram will show that even though the duads move through the entire zodiac within each sign, the first duad of each decanate always coincides with the rulership

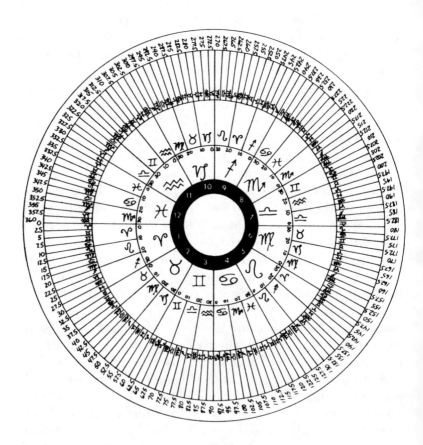

of that decanate. The first decanate of Aries is the Aries decanate, and the first duad in the Aries decanate is the Aries duad. If we look at the second decanate of Aries, or the Leo decanate, we find that the first duad in it is the Leo duad. This pattern is consistent throughout the entire 360 degree wheel. And, this is telling us something. In the same way that the first decanate of every sign reinforces the sign by agreeing with it, so too, the first duad of every decanate reinforces that decanate. Thus, at the beginning of every sign, the sign ruler, the decanate ruler, and the duad ruler are identical. And, at the beginning of every decanate, the decanate ruler and the duad ruler are identical. As a result, signs are strongest within the first 2½ degrees, and decanates are strongest within 2½ degrees of their starting point.

The duads reveal another fascinating concept. We saw how the three cycles of development, creation, destruction, and redemption culminated in water signs. In accordance with nature, water acts as the universal solvent. Thus, whatever is initiated through fire, formed through earth, or transmitted through air can be dissolved through water. There is a difference, however, between cardinal water (Cancer), fixed water (Scorpio) and mutable water (Pisces). In Cancer, the effect of cardinal water manifests through birth as the ultimate symbol of creation. In fact, all birth must occur through water; as the embryonic sac begins its flow towards life. Once life has begun, the human body itself is practically all water. When water cannot flow and becomes fixed, we have the condition we call death (Scorpio), which symbolically completes man's destruction. In Pisces we find the condition of mutable water through which man learns how to accept the ways in which the universe acts on him. Thus, rather than forcing himself into his environment (Cancer) or symbolically leaving it by emotionally negating it (Scorpio) he learns how to blend with his environment through the symbolic redemption of his ego and the acceptance of his role in God's plan for man.

Water is emotion; that quality for which man lives. He can use emotion to create, destroy or redeem. In fact, if whatever he does starts with enthusiasm (Fire) becomes form (Earth) or stimulates thought (Air) it is the water element that will ultimately bring him to the fulfillment that results from the feeling quality of his deeds. The three water signs, then, represent crucial points in man's attempt to reach fulfillment. But, with the understanding that each sign evolves from primitive qualities in its early degrees to more sophisticated awarenesses in its higher degrees, it becomes important to look at the last duad (or 2½ degrees) of each of these water signs. By doing this, we are studying the personal effect of the culmination of a cycle. Interestingly enough, the last duad of each of these water signs is an air sign. The final duad of Cancer, which completes the Creation Cycle, is Gemini. The final duad of Scorpio, which completes the Destruction Cycles is Libra. And, the last duad of Pisces, which completes the Redemption Cycle is Aquarius.

Air symbolizes understanding and one's ability to see the true nature of the universe. It is only through sincerity of emotion (Cancer) and rising above the negative psychic levels (Scorpio) to the purified indwelling stream of clear consciousness (Pisces) that one develops the ability to receive the understanding and awareness that the air signs (which set man above beast) contain. In Gemini man understands creation as duality, but when he is sincerely in touch with his emotions (Cancer) he understands how to enter the hall of wisdom (Gemini) that teaches him how to relate to his environment. In Libra man experiences a world of opposite extremes, but when he emotionally destroys through Scorpio the "twin-minds" of yin and yang that tear him apart, he learns how to achieve harmony of mind. Finally in Aquarius man sees himself as having no personal center. But, when he is emotionally able to sacrifice the illusion of his ego through Pisces, renouncing his pretended control of anything on a personal level, he begins to

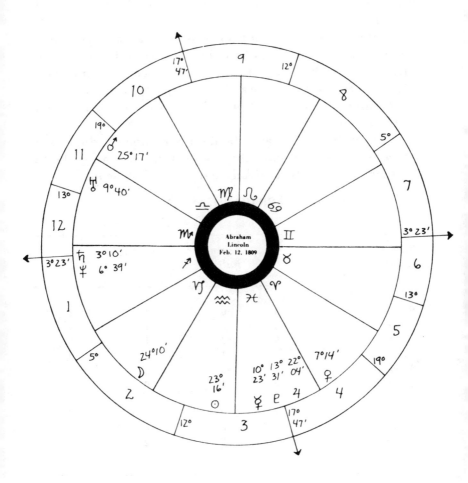

Birth data obtained from "An Astrological Who's Who" by Marc Penfield. Arcance Books, York Harbor, Maine, 1972, p. 288

understand the true nature of how much he is a part of universal mind.

Intellect is above emotion. Most animals are capable of emoting, but it is man in which the gift of thinking is exalted. Still, to reach the awareness that these three different levels of intellect (Gemini, Libra, Aquarius) can bring, one must first experience the emotions of creation, destruction and redemption.

By applying the signs, the decanates, and the duads as a threefold system of rulership, we can discover an in-depth picture of the nature of any particular horoscope.

ABRAHAM LINCOLN

Sign Rulers		Decanate Rulers	Duad Rulers	Total Rulers
Sun:	0	0	2	2
Moon:	0	2	2	4
Mercury:	0	2	1	3
Venus:	1	1	1	3
Mars:	2	3	2	7
Jupiter:	2	2	0	4
Saturn:	1	0	2	3
Uranus:	1	0	1	2
Neptune:	3	0	0	3
Pluto:	1	2	2	5

SUN AT 23′ 16″ of Aquarius, ruled by Uranus (sign) Venus, (decanate) and Mars-Pluto (duad).

In the horoscope of Abraham Lincoln, we find:

First decanate planets:	4
Second decanate planets:	2
Third decanate planets:	4

When we look at the total rulers in Lincoln's chart, we find a fairly even balance except for Mars and Pluto, which may have expressed his involvement in the Civil War. The first and third decanates show an even balance between impulsive action and the wisdom of knowing when and when not to act. Lincoln's wisdom in handling people has been cited by Dale Carnegie as one of the most oustanding examples in history. On one occasion General Meade of the Union army, was able to get the southern forces on the run. He chased them all the way to the banks of a river, and then made camp for the night. Lincoln sent Meade the order to attack immediately. Meade disobeyed the order and while his troops were sleeping, the confederate forces safely escaped across the river. When Lincoln heard this, he wrote a strong letter to General Meade, saying, "I am immeasurably distressed at your failure to take action... this may well have prolonged the war... costing innumerable more lives than necessary..."* Lincoln was prepared to strip Meade of his command. Dale Carnegie asks the question,—What do you think happened with that letter? It was never sent, but instead found among Lincoln's papers after his death.

Here we see the rulerships of his Sun at 23' 16" of Aquarius blending together. Mars-Pluto rules the duad and indicates the desire to take action, possibly even revenge. Uranus ruling the sign indicates that all actions would be tempered with fairness and blending with the Venus rulership of the decanate shows a humane understanding of his fellow man.

The evolution of the sign Aquarius moves through the three decanates, from Uranus through Mercury to Venus, showing how the ability to be impersonal (Uranus) can lead to understanding (Mercury) through which peace (Venus) can ultimately be created. With his Sun in the Libra

---

*"How to Win Friends and Influence People," Dale Carnegie, published by Simon & Schuster, 1936

decanate of Aquarius, not only was the General Meade incident an example of his stiving for peace, but Lincoln's life stood for the (Air element) lesson of Libra as the end of the second cycle of man's development. Libra tries to destroy the concept of twin-minds, double-mindedness and all of the divisions that Gemini creates. Lincoln fought to heal the differences in the nation and to create instead "one nation under God." His Aquarian sign rulership is expressed aptly in his own words,—"that government of the people, by the people, and for the people shall not perish from the earth."

If we look at the modes and elements, we find:

Planets in Cardinal signs:	3
Planets in Fixed signs:	2
Planets in Mutable signs:	5
Planets in Fire signs:	3
Planets in Earth signs:	1
Planets in Air signs:	2
Planets in Water signs:	4

The outstanding mode-element combination is Mutable-Water, which symbolizes the highest refinement of the emotions through the completion of the last water cycle in man's development—his redemption in Pisces. If we try to understand the greatness of such a man, we see his clear vision and perceptiveness symbolized through Mutable-Water energies; the highest emotional purification blended with his Sun in Aquarius. If we look back to nature, we find the sign Aquarius, and the mode-element of mutable water which is in fact, the sign Pisces, symbolizing the compassionate surrender of the past, in order to create a stronger future. Lincoln's life was actually a symbol of the ending of one season in history and its surrender to the next.

The Houses, Hemispheres, and Quadrants

*T*he twelve astrological houses give us a more in depth understanding of what the horoscope is truly saying. Where the signs, decanates and duads show the kind of energies that manifest through a person, the houses indicate those areas in life where these energies will be focused. Thus, there are twelve different kinds of experiences that make up man's totality. And, regardless of what Sun or Moon signs an individual has, it is his house placements within the chart that ultimately show the quality of his life.

Each house is basically analogous to a zodiac sign. We can see this in the diagram below.

SIGN	PLANET RULER	HOUSE
ARIES (self-mastery)	MARS (ego, energy expression)	FIRST HOUSE (personality, physical appearance, identity)

TAURUS (stability, perseverence, wealth, constructive building)	**VENUS** (Ruling an Earth sign) (comfort pleasure)	**SECOND HOUSE** (money, values, resources)
GEMINI (lower mind, duality, communication.)	**MERCURY** (Ruling an Air sign) (conscious thought, adaptability, verbal expression)	**THIRD HOUSE** (relationships, lower education, use of the intellect)
CANCER (home, mother, security, attachment)	**MOON** (emotion, soul, birth) (memory)	**FOURTH HOUSE** (family background roots of the soul, childhood)
LEO (command, creation, brilliant expression)	**SUN** (center of being,the self, creation, energy)	**FIFTH HOUSE** (personal pleasure, children, love affairs investments, creativity)
VIRGO (organization, detail, objects, purification order)	**MERCURY** (Ruling an Earth sign) (concentration, application)	**SIXTH HOUSE** (work, health obligation, service)
LIBRA (love, marriage, harmony, balance)	**VENUS** (Ruling an Air sign) (grace, warmth, softness, delicacy)	**SEVENTH HOUSE** (marriage, alter-ego, partnerships, cooperation)
SCORPIO (sex, death, regeneration, reform, strife)	**MARS** (Ruling a Water sign) **PLUTO** (unconscious energy finding conscious expression)	**EIGHTH HOUSE** (sexual needs, secrets, occult, business, legacy, death, rebirth)
SAGITTARIUS (free-spirit, higher mind, travel, broad vision, luck)	**JUPITER** (higher mind expansion, justice philosophy, the outdoors)	**NINTH HOUSE** (religion, mind-travel, journeys, expansive consciousness)

CAPRICORN (achievement, duty, goals meaning, preservation)	SATURN (the teacher, karma, limits, responsibilities)	TENTH HOUSE (career, social status, direction, peers, adulthood)
AQUARIUS (differences, ingenuity, inventiveness, progress, the future)	URANUS (change, impersonality)	ELEVENTH HOUSE (friendship, hopes, ideals, universal outlook)
PISCES (dreams, romance, e.s.p., fluid perception of life	NEPTUNE (illusions, compassion, impressions, talent mysticism)	TWELFTH HOUSE (completion, fulfillment, hidden understandings, experiences)

The ruling planet, then, symbolizes the basic energy. The sign it rules, filters and focuses this energy so that it can be used. The house shows the areas in which this filtered energy will be applied.

Naturally, houses which have planets in them will receive more attention than those which do not. Still, each of us in one way or another, at different times during our lives experiences something of what each house has to offer.

What is extremely interesting is the yin and yang nature of the houses as they follow each other. All of the odd numbered houses have a Jupiter connotation to them, while the even-numbered houses contain a Saturnian vibration. In this sense, we can see the alternate openness of experiences (Jupiter) and the closed or hidden experiences (Saturn). In the first house, an individual tries to express the personality on the outer world (Jupiter). In the second house we find the inward tapping of one's personal resources along with the attempt to find one's values (Saturn). In the third house, the individual tries to openly communicate what he knows to others (Jupiter), while in the fourth house there tends to be the seeking of inner security through one's home and family (Saturn).

The fifth house (under the rulership of the Sun), is where the individual tries to creatively express all that could possibly emanate from him (Jupiter), while the sixth house indicates not only the inner condition of the body (health), but also the sense of obligation through which one feels impelled to fulfill his duties (Saturn). In the seventh house, we find the optimism of giving through marriage and partnership (Jupiter). The eighth house contains one's sexual secrets and unconscious needs (Saturn). The ninth house (under the natural rulership of Jupiter) shows the ways in which an individual comes into contact with his higher and more expansive perception of reality. The tenth house (under the natural rulership of Saturn) indicates the ways in which one finds his true sense of meaning and belonging (often through some powerful principal that is inwardly ascribed to).

In the eleventh house, there is the expansive concern for humanity as an ideal, along with the open reaching for friends, societies, and the ways in which mankind can experience a more fruitful future (Jupiter).

Finally, in the twelfth house is the culmination or collection of all experiences into the understanding of one's eternal karmic meaning. Through the dissolution of lesser experiences or those whose karmic debts have already been paid, the individual finds his true inner worth (Saturn).

If we can understand the houses from this yin and yang point of view then it will help us in interpretation in terms of understanding why some individuals (containing many planets in odd-numbered houses) lead lives that appear to be quite expansive, reaching outward from the center, and thrusting towards the outer life and all it has to offer. At the same time, individuals with many planets in even-numbered houses seem to pull more of their environment into them as they try to internalize the world. Thus, in one

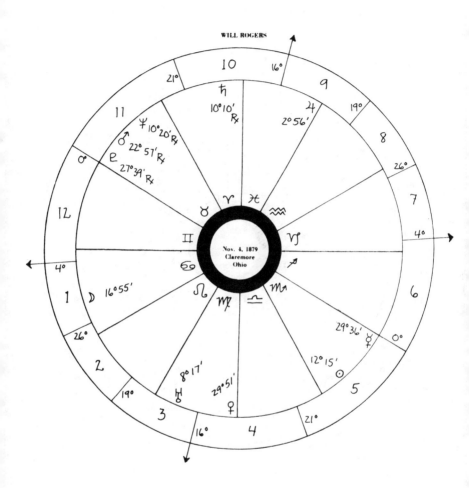

WILL ROGERS

Nov. 4, 1879
Claremore
Ohio

Birth data obtained from "An Astrological Who's Who" by Marc Penfield, Arcane Books, York Harbor, Maine, 1972, p. 406.

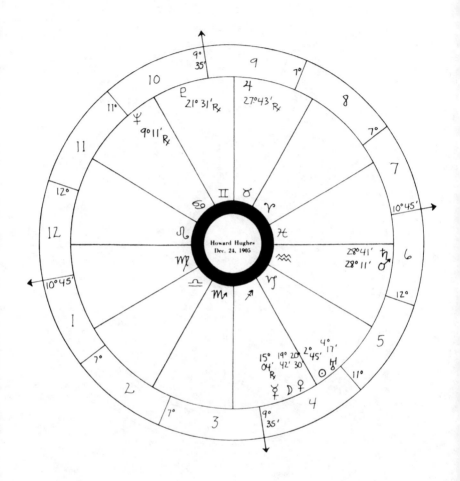

Birth data obtained from "An Astrological Who's Who" by Marc Penfield. Arcane Books, York Harbor, Maine, 1972, p. 219.

case we see an extroverted and expansive lifestyle, while in another, we find more of a closed and self-protective consciousness.

We can see this clearly in the charts of Will Rogers (the traveling humorist), who had 8 planets in odd-numbered houses, and whose life reflected a generous open sense of showmanship, in comparison to Howard Hughes (the billionaire) who through his 9 planets in even-numbered houses preferred to keep his life much of a secluded secret.

Still, what the houses have to tell us does not end here. The number 12 is extremely mystical. It divides each day in half, giving us 6 day houses and 6 night houses. The Ascendant symbolizes the sign coming up to the horizon at sunrise, with each sign taking approximately 2 hours to move 30 degrees. Thus, in 24 hours, each sign of the zodiac is the Ascendant for a 2 hour period. In one sense this accounts for the reason why individuals born at different times in the same day will have different Ascendants and a different arrangement of houses. But, what is more important, is that the half-way point between the day and night houses (or if we were to draw an imaginary line from the Ascendant to the cusp of the seventh house) becomes the horizon; or cleavage line between the upper chart hemisphere (6 day houses) and the lower chart hemisphere (6 night houses).

The Hemispheres

The difference between the day houses and the night houses, in a sense resembles the Jupiter-Saturn analogy we saw earlier between odd and even-numbered houses. The upper hemisphere shows a higher-minded outlook on life. Planets in these 6 day houses reflect the ways in which an individual experiences cosmic meaning, through an open-minded willingness to grow, expand and evolve in tune with mankind. The lower hemisphere shows much more concern with mundane matters on a more personal and intimate basis. The burdens of every-day living are found in the lower hemisphere, while the concern for higher philosophical and more universal meaning is found in the upper hemisphere. Thus, the Jupiter-Saturn analogy has a different meaning here than when we used it in odd and even-numbered houses. To see this, we must view the houses as being contained within the hemispheres. Thus, the difference in hemispheres takes on a larger connotation than the difference from a yin to a yang house within the same hemisphere. An open house in the lower hemisphere (first, third, or fifth) symbolizes more freedom of expression than a closed house within the same hemisphere, but it nevertheless does not experience the cosmic meaning of a closed house in the upper hemisphere. Thus, a Jupiterian house in the lower hemisphere may show a more extroverted outlook than a Saturnian house, but the individual's thoughts, feelings and behavior is still centered within the sphere of mundane consciousness. An open or Jupiterian house in the upper hemisphere (seventh, ninth or eleventh) concerns itself with the higher possibilities of ideas on either an institutional or universal level. Thus, if an individual experiences an altercation with his or her mate through the third house of relationships, there will be an expression of what the person intimately believes to be his point of view. But, if the same altercation is expressed through the seventh house of marriage and partnership (which starts the upper hemisphere) the individual is less expressing his personal point of view than he is his conception of marriage as either an institution or a symbolic representation of what he believes it should be. Practically always, this is a result of his understanding marriage through some society mores or customs that he feels he should live within.

Thus, the difference between the lower and the upper hemisphere is one of consciousness. The day houses in the upper hemisphere are conscious of life as a universal experience. The night houses in the lower hemisphere are basically unconsious of this experience. Often, we refer to the difference between these two hemispheres as the dichotomy between the lower and the higher self. In the lower self (symbolized by the lower hemisphere) man struggles for his personal survival. In the higher self (symbolized by the upper hemisphere) man concerns himself with the part he is playing in the evolution of humanity.

Most horoscopes show planets in both hemispheres. Thus, individuals experience certain parts of life on mundane levels, while they view others on cosmic levels. This is the reason, for example, why Mercury in the third house (where it rules) can easily convey its messages. Mercury is basically concerned with the lower mind, and in this house it finds mundane matters easy to deal with. But, when Mercury appears in the ninth house, the individual is attempting to use his lower mind to understand cosmic matters. As a result, he is often misunderstood. This kind of conflict always occurs when any of the personal planets appear in the upper hemisphere. At the same time, consider the effect of impersonal planets appearing in the lower or mundane hemisphere. In such cases, the individual experiences the difficulty of trying to apply universal theories, ideas and principles to things that are either too small or too mundane to be easily understood as part of the greater cosmic whole. Thus, an individual with Pluto in the Third house tries to communicate personally through the ideas that are prevalent in mass consciousness. This often causes difficulties on mundane levels because people prefer to be spoken to as individuals rather than as symbolic representations of their race.

In addition to the lower and upper hemispheres, the horoscope can be divided in still another way. If we imagine a line (along a somewhat vertical axis) from the fourth house cusp to the tenth house cusp we see two other hemispheres representing the Eastern and Western parts of the chart. Usually students tend to confuse this separation, however, because of the accustomed tendency to equate

West to the left hemisphere and East to the right hemisphere. We must remember that the chart is a map of the heavens rather than the earth. Thus, the left hemisphere is East and the right hemisphere is West.

When the horoscope is divided this way, we have three day houses and three night houses in each hemisphere. Thus, in both the East and the West the individual experiences both the mundane and the cosmic part of life approximately equal. The Eastern hemisphere (left side of the chart) represents midnight progressing towards noon, while the Western hemisphere (right side of the chart) indicates the progression from noon to the following midnight. Thus, the left side of the chart shows what an individual experiences as the Sun is rising; from its weakest position at midnight to its full strength at noon. Since the Sun holds rulership over the power of the Self, this left hemisphere shows the ways in which an individual has some control over his life experiences. The right hemisphere represents the progression of the Sun moving from full strength at noon to its apparent weakest strength at midnight. Likewise, here the power of the Self wanes and is replaced by the ways in which the individual must depend upon others and his environment to complete his experiences. As a result of this, the amount of planets in either the left or right hemispheres show just how much an individual has control over his life or how much he must share that control with others. In the three night houses of the left hemisphere, the individual may exert control over his mundane existence. In the three day houses in this same hemisphere, the person can even experience a certain amount of control over his cosmic or universal experiences. When we look at the right (or Western) hemisphere we find the individual's reactions to life on a mundane or social level (in the three night houses) and on a collective level (in the three day houses). Thus, we find the lower self that can exert control and the lower self that does not have complete control in the left and right sides of the lower hemisphere.

We also find the higher self that can experience control and the higher self that must cooperatively experience its environment and society in the left and right sides of the upper hemisphere. This means that we can actually divide the horoscope into two sets of hemispheres approximately perpendicular to each other. He must not only learn how to please others, but also how to earn their personal cooperation if he is to fulfill his needs. This second quadrant, then, is called the *social* quadrant.

In the third quadrant (houses seven, eight and nine) we find the combination of the upper hemisphere and the right hemisphere. Here an individual must learn how to cooperate with external forces that are larger than himself. He must function amidst things that he often does not fully understand and cannot completely control. Still, he must accept his role an impersonal part of mass consciousness. His experiences are a product of ideas that he personally may have played no role in shaping. His interaction with life may well be strongly influenced by present or past civilizations that have shaped the world in ways which he can do little to change. Thus, in this part of the horoscope, man behaves in accordance with the opinions, attitudes, morals, customs, and historic folklore, legends and traditions that confront him everywhere in mass consciousness. This third quadrant, then, can be aptly called, the *collective* quadrant.

Finally, in the fourth quadrant (houses ten, eleven and twelve) we find the upper hemispher combining with the left hemisphere. Here, man is able to exert control over his cosmic Self. Rising to his full state of being, he may throw off the shackles of personal subjectivity, social sacrifice, collective influence and the attitudes and opinions of his environment. By so doing, he can attain self-realization in the cosmic universe he perceives. Thus, he is no longer a slave to himself or others, or even the society in which he lives, but rather he can become in tune with his cosmic state of being. When he does this, he realizes his true universal nature. This fourth quadrant, then, can be called the *cosmic* quadrant.

The Quadrants

When this is done, we have four quadrants containing exactly three houses each. And, because each quadrant has a hemisphere classification (i.e. lower or upper, East or West) we are able to see the horoscope as symbolizing four important cycles of human experience. In the first quadrant (houses one, two and three) we find the combined effect of the left hemisphere (action) and the lower hemisphere (lower self). Thus, these are the houses through which the individual learns to master his personal self. He deals with mundane matters through a subjective viewpoint and tries to discover his intimate relationship with himself. As he copes with identity crises, growing and changing values, and the lessons he learns in closely relating to others, he begins to understand the nature of the "lower self." He may find himself experiencing different aspects of his personality, including character traits that other parts of him seem to be above. Yet, only through this quadrant does he get the opportunity to know and understand his lower self intimately. He is basically a product of his actions as he tries to impress himself on the outside world. The cardinal quality of the first house, followed by the fixed quality of the second house, and ultimately ending the quadrant in the mutable quality of the third house shows how actions are first expressed, then sustained and considered afterward. Since the first house is like the sign, Aries, and the third house is like Gemini, we can easily understand how lower self impulses (Aries) thrust towards physical expression (Taurus) and then must reach understanding (Gemini). Thus, the experiences of the lower self are rarely if ever, thought followed by action, but are rather the expression of primitive impulses and drives which lead to duality of mind (third house) when the lower self tries to reach its understandings. Because these first three houses show the ways in which lower self expression thrusts towards action, we call this section of the horoscope the *personal* quadrant.

In the second quadrant (houses four, five and six) we find the combined effects of the lower hemisphere (lower self) and the right hemisphere (reaction). Here, the individual relates to his environment and struggles for his survival. He experiences the conflicts between his needs and the imposing needs of others in a series of circumstances and situations in which he must make compromises. The more he can fulfill the needs of his family, his children and his superiors, the more adaptable he grows in ultimately gaining mastery over his environment. In this quadrant, he feels how much others who are close to him can impinge on his personal freedom and he keeps going through decisions which help him cope with the changing needs in others that he is expected to meet. This is often viewed as a difficult quadrant, for the lower self cannot act freely of its own accord but instead must often take on a more social, tactful, and sometimes even a defensive quality in order to preserve its identity. Thus, here the individual learns not only how to share and cooperate with others, but also how to react appropriately in the mundane world that he cannot exert control over. This second quadrant, then, is called the *social* quadrant.

In the third quadrant (houses seven, eight and nine) we find the combination of the right hemisphere (reaction) and the upper hemisphere (higher self). Here the individual learns how to accept his role as an impersonal part of mass consciousness. His experiences are a product of ideas that he personally may have played no role in shaping. His interaction with life may well be strongly influenced by present or past civilizations that have shaped the world in ways which he can do little to change. Thus, he behaves in accordance with the opinions, attitudes, morals, customs, historic folklore, legends and traditions that confront him everywhere through collective consciousness. Through his higher self, he reacts to religion, the beliefs of others, and the values of the society he lives in. This quadrant differs from the second quadrant insomuch as here the individual is reacting to things that are far less close to him but still exert a strong influence over his freedom of thought. Thus, although he may feel that marriage, sexuality and philosophy (seventh, eighth and ninth houses) are personal to him, they really reflect the ways in which he is a symbolic product of a greater collective whole within whose framework his experiences are contained. Whatever he does, in some small measure, contributes to the collective consciousness, but he is more shaped by what already exists than by whatever degree he could possibly exert any substantial change over it. This quadrant then, is called the *collective* quadrant.

In the fourth quadrant (houses ten, eleven and twelve) we find the left hemisphere (action) combining with the upper hemisphere (higher self). Here man learns to establish control over his cosmic identity. Rising to his full state of being, he may throw off the shackles of personal subjectivity, social sacrifice, collective influence and the attitudes and opinions of his environment. Thus, he is no longer a slave to himself or others, or even the society in which he lives, but rather can become in tune with his own divine nature. Here, one learns how to act in accordance with cosmic law, the ebb and flow of natural forces, and ultimately comes to understand the creative principle. The sense of identification is not personal, but rather comes through the individual realizing that he is neither less nor more than one drop of water (which is neither different or the same as every drop) in the ocean of God. For this reason, we call this section of the horoscope, the *cosmic* quadrant.

The Conscious Self—The Unconscious Self

The two quadrants in the upper hemisphere symbolize the thoughts, feelings and actions of the conscious Self.

Here the individual is aware of his relationship with his environment. Through his higher self, he is fully conscious of his role in humanity's evolutionary process. Thus, he participates in life through experiences which symbolically reveal his contribution to mass consciousness. In this way, he is able to consciously perceive reasons for his existence as well as tolerance for the existence of all else in the world.

The conscious self is filled with awarenesses; gleaning knowledge and reaping the harvest of all that is available in a growing and changing world. Unfettered by personal burdens, it perceives the lower or unconscious self as a necessary, but not all important part of life. Thus, the higher conscious self lives for more than individualism. It seeks to find the niche in the world through which it can do the most good for others, and its own evolution as an example for others.

Negative personal motivations, such as greed, envy, possessiveness and fear are not part of the conscious self's makeup. These kind of feelings emanate from the lower unconscious self, which because it cannot perceive the higher conscious self clearly, feels the limits of its existence. It never realizes that there truly is more to life than expending one's energy to see how much in the form of possessions or achievements it can magnetize to itself. In reality, the lower self can only expand to the limits of the higher self's function. Thus, if the higher self is "sleeping" (not consciously perceiving its role in society and humanity), then the life experiences of the lower unconscious self will be rather closed, small and confined. When the higher conscious self is blossoming in all of the ways that it can realize its positive relationship with everything, then the life experiences of the lower self must be large and plentiful enough to support it.

What is important to realize, is that although the possibilities and potentials of the higher self are more exciting to contemplate than the mundane activities of the unconscious lower self, one cannot truly exist without the other. Spiritual awakenings are fruitless unless we can bring them down to everyday reality and find the ways in which they can make the mundane world a sweeter place in which to live. At the same time, it is only through observation of the lower unconscious self, that the higher conscious self learns how to become more in tune with an ever-growing set of cosmic or collective principles which enhance life's beauty and contribute to its meaning.

If we think of the first six signs of the zodiac (from Aries through Virgo) as being analogous to the first six houses, then the true nature of the lower unconscious self becomes clear. Aries (ruled by Mars) symbolizes the primitive impulses emanating from the personal identity. Virgo, (under the rulership of Mercury) completes this hemisphere as it symbolizes service to the self. Thus, the entire lower hemisphere is unconscious of a larger existence than it can perceive because its viewpoint is limited by a great deal of self-absorption.

The upper hemisphere, however, is analogous to the last six signs of the zodiac (from Libra through Pisces). Thus, it begins with the concept of cooperation, sharing, and the giving of love, and progresses from the rulership of Venus to the rulership of Neptune (Pisces) where compassion, divine love, and a mystical and cosmic understanding of the world symbolically take place. The awareness that expands consciousness in the upper hemisphere then, becomes possible not only because the attention is not focused on the self, but specifically because there is an outpouring of love and the sharing of understandings with humanity.

Most charts have some planets in the upper hemisphere and some planets in the lower hemisphere. If we think of natural rulerships, five of the six houses (and their corresponding signs) in the upper hemisphere are ruled by outer, or co-conscious planets. Jupiter, Saturn, Uranus, Neptune and Pluto all find their natural rulerships in this conscious part of the chart.

What is interesting to observe is those charts where the outer planets (which symbolize consciousness) appear in the lower hemisphere (the unconscious part of the horoscope) and vice versa. Where this occurs, the individual must learn how to blend the conscious and the unconscious into a harmonious life experience. Often this is not an easy thing to do. Consider for example, the placement of Neptune in the second house. Here, the planetary energy is foreign to the quality of the house experiences. Neptune (at its home in the last house or sign of the upper hemisphere—Pisces) compassionately pours its love, but in the confines of the personal quality of the second house, this can easily become a possessive imagination with a martyr-like attitude towards money. Thus, the higher self qualities of Neptune can easily be perverted by the lower-self experiences it must go through in the second house. Similar difficulties occur when any of the planets ruling lower-self unconscious signs appear in any of the conscious houses of the upper hemisphere. To see this, consider the action of Mercury (at home in Gemini—third house, and enhanced or exalted in Virgo—sixth house) attempting to personalize through the lower mind ninth house experiences which are not personal at all. Of course it would be extremely rare to see horoscopes that have all of the outer planets in the upper hemisphere and all of the personal (inner) planets in the lower hemisphere. Thus, it is more common to realize the different conflicts that individuals experience between their higher and lower self through their planet placements which do not fall in the appropriate hemisphere. In a way, these placements could be considered as a link between the conscious and the unconscious, for they afford the individual the opportunity to experience both in relation to each other.

The Sign Quadrants

Although tradition derives the quadrants from the houses, we can learn much more about the horoscope by realizing that there is actually another set of quadrants. Since the planets which hold rulership over the houses also hold rulership over the signs which they are analogous to, there is a direct relationship between the houses and the signs which becomes important to study. Mars rules the first house, but it also rules the first sign—Aries. Venus rules the second house, but it also rules the second sign—Taurus. Mercury rules the third house, but it also rules the third sign—Gemini. Thus, the three planets which rule the first quadrant (derived from houses) also rule the first three signs (or first quarter) of the zodiac.

As a result, we can see the formation of a quadrant (derived from these personal signs. The next three signs (Cancer, Leo, Virgo) will form the second sign quadrant. And, because of their social nature (similar to the social nature of houses four, five and six) these signs also form a quadrant. The third sign quadrant is made up of the signs, Libra, Scorpio and Sagittarius (similar to houses seven, eight and nine). These signs show collective interest expressed through a desire to smooth, reform and bring to truth the thoughts and ideas in mass consciousness. Finally, the signs, Capricorn, Aquarius and Pisces (similar to the last three houses—ten, eleven and twelve) complete the final quadrant. In these signs, one's higher state of being is reached for through struggle leading to understanding and culminating in awareness.

To understand the essence of these sign quadrants, we must clearly know the difference between the action of a planet, a sign and a house. Planets represent energies, basically raw and undifferentiated. The zodiac signs act as filters which put boundaries and limits on how the planet energies will work. Thus, a planet in one sign will have its energies filtered differently than a planet in another sign. Then, the filtered energy is directed through a house towards some area of life experience. To see this, consider Venus in Aries. Basically, the planetary energy is one of love, softness and harmony. Aries filters this energy, adding a great deal of stamina to it and focusing it on self-expression. If this configuration appears in the third house, the self-expression will find its outlet through the experiences of communication, learning and short journeys. On the other hand, if Venus in Aries appears in the fourth house, the love for self-expression will be manifested through the family. In this way, the signs show us the filtered energy while the houses point to where such energy will be applied.

This distinction becomes important if we try to consider the difference between a system of quadrants formed from the houses and a system of quadrants derived from the signs.

When we look at traditional house quadrants, the first quadrant will always begin at the Ascendant and include the first three houses. Naturally, in each horoscope, the Ascendant differs. Thus, from one chart to another the first quadrant will have different signs in it.

But, when we look at a system of quadrants derived from the signs themselves the first quadrant will always begin with the sign Aries, regardless of where it appears in any particular horoscope. This means that in any given chart we have an actual overlay of two systems of quadrants, which may line up with each other in a variety of different ways. As a result, each planet in the chart can be in one sign quadrant while being in a totally different house quadrant at the same time.

To understand how this works, study the chart on page 158 which shows the house quadrants lined up with the sign quadrants. First see how each quadrant expresses the half-hemisphere it is located in. Then, imagine what would happen with different signs rising.

Consider a horoscope with Gemini rising. Instead of Aries (the first sign of Spring) appearing in the first house (personal identity), it appears as the middle sign of the fourth quadrant (cosmic being). We noted in an earlier chapter how the middle sign of each natural season must sustain the season through the Fixed mode. In this chart,

THE QUADRANTS

—CONSCIOUS—

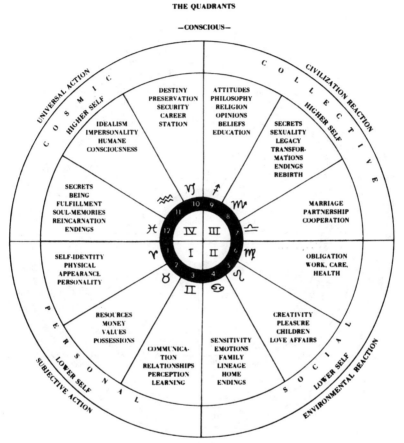

—UNCONSCIOUS—

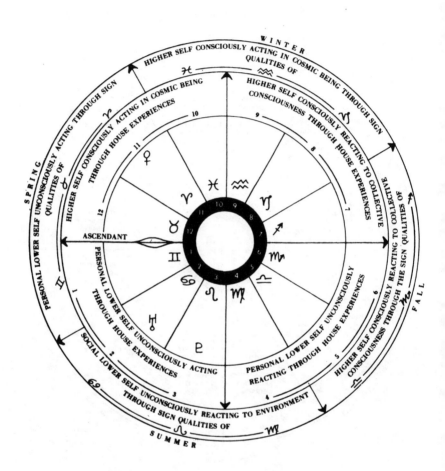

the individual must find fixed qualities in Aires (a Cardinal sign) if he is to sustain his sense of cosmic being. Although this appears difficult, it can be achieved by consistently meeting the challenges that reaffirm one's cosmic essence. Still this is not the only difficulty in this type of chart.

The first quadrant is made up of one personal sign (Gemini) and two social signs (Cancer and Leo). Thus, when we study the first house (Gemini) we find an overlapping of our two systems of quadrants. As the individual tries to seek his identity (Gemini in the first house), he is personally acting out the inquisitive nature of the sign (Gemini in the first sign quadrant). At the same time, because he is unaware of what he is asking (unconscious hemisphere) he invites the kind of experiences into his life (Gemini in the first quadrant derived from houses) that give him dualistic answers. Thus, on a very personal intimate level he is never quite sure of himself.

What makes this more complex is that the next two signs in the first quadrant (derived from houses) are really what we might call borrowed signs from the natural second quadrant. As a result, what the individual feels he can easily act out on a personal level (second and third house in the first quadrant of personal action) become thwarted through the sign qualities of Cancer and Leo. These two signs must respond to social environment. As a result, the individual experiences his first quadrant of personal unconscious actions through the lower self in a dualistic way. Although he may believe that his experiences symbolize his personal beliefs and ideas, he is only the role-player in his identity (Gemini in the first house); for his values (second house— Cancer) and the ways in which he relates to others (third house—Leo) are more a function of his reactions to those close to him than they are the free expression of his personal self. In this kind of chart then, we find the lower personal self (first quadrant) going through the yin and yang experiences and qualities of expression which create a sense of dual identity.

When we interpret the meaning of Uranus in Cancer in the second house, our system of quadrant overlays can show us the clear significance of this placement.

Uranus is the planet of "change." Its hectic and unpredictable vibration must first filter through the sign Cancer and then meet with the experiences of the second house.

In its natural condition, Uranus is an impersonal planet. It rules Aquarius—the symbolic Grand Man of the future. When placed in the lower hemisphere, Uranus tends to depersonalize the personal qualities of the individual. In the sign Cancer, its vibration of change acts to create emotional changes through depersonalization. This causes conflict. The basic quality of Cancer is "attachment." The basic quality of Uranus is "detachment." Thus, the individual experiences both in a yin and yang battle that constantly shows him these two extremes.

Although Cancer appears in the second house (natural first quadrant derived from houses), it is basically a second quadrant sign (based on sign quadrants). Thus, the qualities of the sign Cancer must be seen as how the individual emotionally reacts to those close to him. Keeping this in mind, we see the conflict of the individual attempting to earn money for himself (second house) while in fact, he is reacting to the needs of others. Thus, if we are to clearly interpret the placement of Uranus in Cancer in the second house, we must see how the impersonal action of the planet first stimulates personal emotion through the sign (Cancer) which ultimately manifests in the ways the individual's lower self establishes its resources by unconsciously reacting to the actions of others. As a result, this placement of an impersonal planet in a personal sign which socially reacts, will always manifest through unconscious actions in attempts to make up for reactions.

This placement shows how the lower self, reacting to the past (Uranus in Cancer) tries to secure its future (Uranus in the second house).

In formulating our interpretations of planets-signs, and houses, all we have to do is note how each is integrating with the other within the structure of the quadrant or quadrants that it appears.

To take this analogy further, our sample horoscope shows Pluto in Leo in the third house. As the natural ruler of Scorpio, Pluto is at home in the third quadrant. There it can unconsciously react to mass consciousness and symbolically represent influences of generations, collective movements, and race evolution. In the first quadrant, however, these impersonal transformations that mankind experiences on its evolutionary path are taken personally. Leo is naturally at home in the second quadrant (as the fifth sign of the zodiac). There it helps man to cope with the powerful forces in his environment that he must constantly deal with. In the first quadrant, however, the reactive qualities of Leo as a sign are unconsciously taken on a personal level. The individual thinks that in some way he must compete with or combat the strength in his environment that is actually in himself. When we combine the planet and the sign, (Pluto in Leo), we find the individual unconsciously reacting to power in others—both on a social (Leo) level, and a collective (Pluto) level.

These reactions, however are part of the first quadrant (derived from houses). Thus, what the individual thinks (third house) are his reactions to forces outside of himself are truly part of the actions he uses in expressing his unconscious lower self. Since the planet must first act through the sign, and then be expressed through a house experience, the individual is first reacting (Pluto in Leo) to others and their collective power, and then experiencing his own ideas (third house). Thus, in this instance, we have the rather unique occurence of reaction coming before action.

An individual with Pluto in Leo in the third house will feel the struggle of humanity as it evolves through extremes. He will take collective ideas personally, and also experience the desire to be free from power that may not even be exerted on him. Thus, his actions (on a purely personal level) will be based on the sizeable force he believes he has to overcome in order to express his beliefs. This often results in a powerful communicator, personally concerned with social and collective transformations.

We often find in charts certain perculiar inconsistencies that make us wonder what is the real truth about an individual's nature. If we study each planet, sign and house placement through our two-fold system of quadrants, these inconsistencies clear up.

In our example, we also see Venus in Aries in the Eleventh House. This is often interpreted as self-love or an exemplification of narcissism. But, does it not seem inconsistant that a narcissistic person would be so overly concerned with social or collective reform? Perhaps. Let us study this placement in detail to see its meaning.

The basic energy of Venus is love. When this is expressed through the qualities of Aries, there tends to be a focus of attention on the self. But, the eleventh house is naturally impersonal, and often cares more for the needs of others than for the self. Thus, we see a very basic conflict in the possible ways this planetary placement could manifest. This becomes clearer when we examine the quadrants. Aries starts the first sign quadrant. It symbolizes the ways the lower self seeks to unconsciously (and often primitively) express its needs through the ego. The life experiences it meets with, however, are not only impersonal (eleventh house) but also reflect what the higher self needs to experience in order to act in its true cosmic nature. As a result, the individual with this placement may personally seek to gain the love and admiration of groups and societies that work for the public gain and the evolution of humanity. Thus, the more the person seeks self-love and personal aggrandizement (Venus in Aries, first sign quadrant), the more he achieves a conscious awareness of being an effective instrument in the progress of humanity. This placement carries with it the rather unique characteristic blending the lower and the higher self. Through the experiences in consciousness of the eleventh house, the individual ultimately comes to understand that the self-worth that his lower self is unconsciously seeking can be obtained only through personally identifying with all that symbolizes the public good.

When we see this it becomes easy to understand how a certain amount of narcissistic self-love and a concern with social reform can be harmoniously blended with the same individual.

Individuals relate to their life experiences differently. Sometimes, things which are basically personal are seen through either a social or collective viewpoint. Sometimes individuals become personally attached to cosmic or universal truths that they feel are important to them. We even find instances in which the collective truths of organizations become personalized. And, we find much world confusion when action and reaction get distorted.

By moving the inner wheel in the chart on page 158, we can see all of the different possible ways in which the houses and signs could line up with each other. Consider, an individual with Pisces rising. This puts the last sign quadrant overlapping the first house quadrant. As a result, the individual must use *cosmic* energy (Pisces) for dealing with *personal* reality (first house). Only by unselfishly functioning through the higher conscious self, can this individual fulfill the needs of the personality.

One of the most fascinating possible horoscopes is the Libra rising chart. Here we find all of the signs attempting to manifest through house experiences that are exactly opposite their natural qualities. Thus, in the first house, the basic ego is a reaction to the collective ego. The individual feels the Cardinal initiatory energy of the first house and tries to personally express their will on a world whose collective higher self forces them to make compromises. In the second house of constructive resources, we find the sign, Scorpio which carries with it a great deal of destructive energy. All throughout the wheel of this kind of a chart we see the ways in which the individual perceives the world as opposite the qualities of energy that they are trying to express.

The individual with Sagittarius rising will unconsciously act in accordance with his conscious reactions to the *collective* consciousness. Thus, much of what he believes is personal is truly his reactions to impersonal ideas that society is based on.

The student would do well to study each rising sign, and the ways possible planetary placements in different houses act through the quadrants. In this way, the specific meaning of each placement can easily be interpreted.

The Beginning of Chart
Delineation

*N*ow that we have many of our basic tools, we are ready to apply our knowledge to an actual chart. In the horoscope of Ernest Hemingway, we find 7 planets in the left hemisphere. Thus, his life would have been one of actions emanating from the lower and higher self. His 3 planets in the *social* quadrant show a sensitivity to others and his ability to react to their ideas. But, the *collective* quadrant is empty. Thus, he would not have been very much influenced by thoughts, opinions or attitudes in the collective quadrant that did not directly apply to his own intentions. This showed up in his lifestyle, for he was basically unconventional and hardly motivated by the traditions and customs of society.

If we use our two-fold system of quadrants, we find that his first sign quadrant begins in the Ninth House in Aries. Interestingly enough, Hemingway was a strong nature lover (ruled by this house). Through his ability to personalize the outdoors, he brought much feeling and vividness into his writing. The Ninth House indicates writing from the higher mind, publishing and expressing opinions that come from the natural environment. It is important to realize then, that this house starts the *personal* quadrant (derived from signs) in Hemingway's chart.

In this same quadrant, we find both Pluto and Neptune (the two outer planets symbolizing the end of both the destruction and redemption cycles—as rules of Scorpio and Pisces) in Gemini (the sign of writing) in the Tenth House of career. Interestingly enough, Neptune rules water, and one of Hemingway's greatest books was "The Old Man and the Sea." This Neptune in Gemini in the Tenth House placement would have to work in the order of planet-sign-house. Thus, first we understand the meaning of Neptune (imagination, impressions, intuition, dreams) in Gemini (commmunication, stories, messages). Then, by realizing that Gemini is part of the first sign quadrant that Hemingway would have taken his career seriously enough to personally identify with it. Gemini symbolizes an analogy to the natural Third House. Thus, through Gemini in the Tenth, the author would have been expressing his most intimate viewpoints of life and the ways in which he related to it. At the same time, the Tenth House begins the fourth or *cosmic* house quadrant. Thus, Hemingway's creative imagination would have been both personal and cosmic at the same time. One could read his stories and feel deep personal messages in them, and still sense a greater meaning that has more to do with man's cosmic essence.

With the Sun and Venus in Cancer, Hemingway had a great ability to feel emotions. But, because these two planets appear in the Eleventh House (under the natural rulership of Aquarius) he could understand universal emotion. Cancer is naturally part of the *social* sign quadrant, and its placement here would show the ability to react to one's personal environment; deeply understanding the feelings of others, while still retaining an Eleventh House universality and detached outlook.

With four planets in the Destruction cycle, one of Hemingway's favorite themes was man's eternally damned struggle against forces he could not control. Even his own

ERNEST HEMINGWAY
July 21, 1899
Oak Park, Ill.

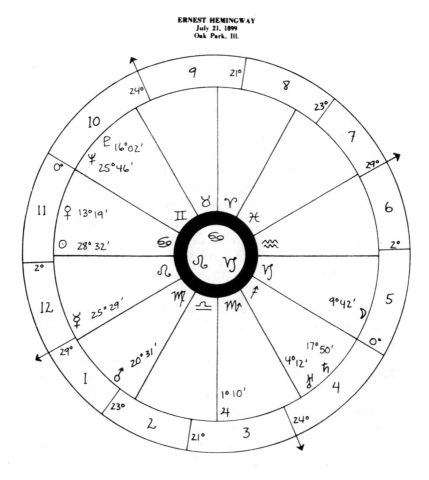

Birth data obtained from "An Astrological Who's Who" by Marc Penfield. Arcane
Books, York Harbor, Maine, 1972, p. 219.

lifestyle reflected the ruggedness of struggle for survival. *For Whom The Bell Tolls* is typical of the Jupiter in Scorpio placement in the Third House. Here, he shows a sense of mystical justice in man's idea of his relationship with himself.

The Capricorn Moon in the Fifth House is in its detriment, indicating difficulty in freely expressing emotions. Here, Hemingway would have felt the conflict between feelings he could know about (Venus in Cancer in the Eleventh House) and easily put into his writing, and his own emotional reactions in his personal life (Moon in Capricorn—lower chart hemisphere).

His Mercury in Leo placement falls in the third decanate of the sign (Aries decan), thus indicating how much his conscious concentration would be focused on individuality and autonomous survival.

Now that we have looked at some of the outstanding characteristics in the chart, it becomes important to use a systematic method that will help us from overlooking details that are significant.

Once a preliminary study of the chart is done, the best method for delineation is to proceed house by house in order. By doing this, the chart develops itself, unfolding through the natural progression of the quadrants and houses until it completes itself in the Twelfth House.

The Leo Ascendant starts the *personal* house quadrant, indicating a sense of flare and flamboyancy to his character. Virgo, Libra and Scorpio complete this quadrant, putting the *destruction* cycle in the personal area. Thus, in his private existence, Hemingway would personally feel man's innate struggles. Mars in Virgo appears in the First House, showing the ego (Mars) filtering through the understanding of how things work. An attention to detail, along with a strong interest in seeing how man seeks order amidst destruction (Mars is also the co-ruler of Scorpio) is found in this placement.

Virgo starts the cusp of the Second House. Under the exaltation of Mercury (placed in Leo in the Twelfth House—under the natural rulership of Neptune appearing in Gemini), we find how much the value systems, resources, and finances would depend upon writing (Mercury in Gemini), understanding the order of things (Virgo) and a higher intuitive sense of how to express creativity (Mercury in Leo in the Twelfth House). It is important to see at this point, that when we study the rulership of a House, it can lead us to other areas in the chart that are related to it. Thus, in this case, Mercury's exaltation of Virgo is only part of the explanation of the Second House. Whatever else Mercury is doing in the chart along with the ways the other sign it rules relates to the House it is in completes the picture of Mercury's influence. Thus, Neptune in Gemini is related to Mercury in the Twelfth House because Neptune rules the Twelfth House and Gemini is under the rulership of Mercury.

Whenever a planet in a sign is the reverse of another planet in another sign through rulerships, we call it Mutual Reception. But, it is important to understand that mutual reception (indicating how two different chart placements can actually help each other) can also occur through the more subtle relationship of a planet in a sign being related to a planet in a house. Thus, in this chart we see the latter relationship, helping to strengthen the influence of Mercury (the planet of writers).

The Third House starts in Libra and has Jupiter in Scorpio in it. Venus, the ruler of the sign on the cusp is in Cancer in the Eleventh House, where under the natural rulership of Aquarius we can refer to its ruler; Uranus in Sagittarius in the Fourth House. Hemingway wrote with a great amount of love and feeling (Libra Third House), (Venus in Cancer), but his writing was also extremely passionate (Jupiter in Scorpio in the Third House). The Uranus influence not only shows that his writing was his gift to mankind (Sun in the Eleventh House), but also how much he wanted to make people aware of nature (Uranus in Sagittarius). Thus, he would view his personal relationship to himself (Third House) and the things he wanted to communicate to others as a gift of passionate love to the ever-reaching higher self of humanity (Uranus in Sagittarius—both naturally at home in the upper chart hemisphere.) What is interesting is that Hemingway had Jupiter in its fall in the Third House. We often tend to misguide our thinking into believing with this placement. Yet, it did not stop Hemingway from his most effective writing. He could show man the relationship (Third House) between the collective ideas in civilization (Jupiter—Third quadrant) and the unconscious personal struggle (Scorpio in the Third House) that individuals go through to achieve understanding.

This first quadrant is made up of two *social* signs and two *collective* signs. Thus, because the *social* and *collective* quadrants represent the Western or Reaction hemisphere, and they must manifest through the *personal* quadrant,— Hemingway's intimate existence would have been an expression of the ways in which he could integrate *social* and *collective* reactions to externals with all he could achieve through *personal* action. As we saw earlier, having no planets in the *collective* quadrant, he could have had some difficulty in relating intimately to this area. But, the Jupiter in Scorpio placement helps to balance this lack.

Hemingway's fourth house starts in Scorpio. Here we find the emotions at the very core of one's soul. Pluto, the ruler is in Gemini, showing the depth of feeling that would be put into writing. Uranus and Saturn both in Sagittarius in the Fourth House indicate the finding of a home away from home, a deep emotional attraction to the outdoors, and a dedication to discoveries through the use of the higher mind. The Fourth House starts the *social* quadrant (derived from houses), while Scorpio and Sagittarius here both show an influence from the *collective* quadrant (derived from signs). Thus, his home environment, emotional roots, and foundations, would have been deeply sensitive not only to the needs of those close to him, but also to ideas in consciousness that he had no personal role in shaping. Hemingway had a feel for mankind. Somehow he knew what prompts, motivates and inspires man. And, he got most of his knowledge from his intimate relationship with nature (Sagittarius in the Fourth). The placement of Saturn in Sagittarius shows an ability to teach higher philosophic lessons. In his book, *The Old Man and the Sea*, Hemingway told of the struggle to catch a prize-winning fish that was ultimately lost. But, the moral he points to is that the idea of winning the struggle can often be greater or more important than the prize itself.

The Capricorn Moon in the Fifth House shows that with all of Hemingway's great thirst for life, he did in fact take his creative impulses seriously. The message of Capricorn is that one of the best ways to spend one's life is on something that will outlast it. Thus, in his emotional structure, Hemingway would have been thinking beyond himself and beyond his personal feelings. Capricorn naturally begins the fourth or *cosmic* sign quadrant, and would have made Hemingway emotionally react to man's greater reasons for being.

The Sixth House completes the lower hemisphere and symbolizes man's service to himself. With Aquarius here, the author could easily have felt that the greatest he could do for himself would be to experience personal freedom. The ruler, Uranus is in Sagittarius which would account for Hemingway liking to find places in the woods or distant countrysides to do his writing. As this House describes working conditions, we see the need to seek unique environments as settings in which his soul (Uranus in Sagittarius in the Fourth House) could unfold itself.

The Seventh House of marriage begins the upper chart hemsiphere, symbolizing the beginning of consciousness of the higher self. Hemingway had several marriages (a commonplace occurrence with Aquarius here), but more important is his sense of freedom of mind in conscious relationships with others. Aquarius is naturally at home in the Eleventh House. Thus, we find a *cosmic* or fourth quadrant influence expressing itself through the Seventh House. Here, the soul's wish to be free struggles against the bindings of any marriage which might be restrictive.

In the Eighth House, we find the sign Pisces, under the natural rulership of Neptune. This house often shows us how the individual relates to the values of others. Pisces is intuitive, compassionate and sensitive. Neptune in Gemini is a veritable artist at understanding the ideas of others. In his third quadrant, the *collective* ideas that Hemingway would hear of, or feel, could be raised to higher *cosmic* levels through the Piscean influence, which naturally relates to the Twelfth House (the fulfillment of man's greater essence).

The Aries Ninth House (which completes the third quadrant) we saw earlier showing the connection between the author's personal identification and his relationship with the great outdoors. We can see this even stronger through the connection to Mars (the ruler of Aries) in the first house of personal identity. Hemingway loved personal challenges, battles against nature, and feeling like he was a natural part of the ebb and flow of countrysides, trees, and secluded bodies of water. This Aries Ninth House shows individualism at its zenith.

The Tenth House begins the last or *cosmic* quadrant. We saw how the Neptune and Pluto placements here brought a higher conscious awareness to his writing. It is also important to understand that Pluto rules mass consciousness. An individual with Pluto in the Tenth House will undoubtedly work towards the evolution of mankind in some manner or another. Here, the values of others as expressed through collective consciousness (Pluto as natural ruler of the Eighth House) blend with the need for personal communication (Gemini as natural ruler of the Third

House) to meet with a sense of destiny (Tenth House). Interestingly enough, this Tenth House starts with Taurus; the physical earth sign which is so sensitive to scenery, color, and the absorbtion of love from the natural environment.

The Eleventh House starts in Cancer. This House is of particular importance because it contains Hemingway's Sun. Under the Aquarian rulership of this House, the Sun in Cancer directs its sense of nourishment outwardly towards humanity. It seeks a universal home in which man feels free because he is attached to all that has feeling for him. Sensitivity is blended with the higher intellect into a sense of fairness in dealing with all that is new. Here, the *cosmic* house quadrant combines with the *social* sign quadrant, indicating *cosmic* actions and *social* reactions. All the ways in which the lower self emotionally reacts to its environment (Sun in Cancer—Fourth House in Scorpio/Sagittarius) provide the stepping stones for the higher self (Sun in the Eleventh House) to exhude all that its intellect can comprehend. Thus, personal fulfillment through being able to absorb the natural environment, enabled Hemingway to convey his great sense of wonder through his books.

The Twelfth House starts in Leo and contains Mercury within it. We saw the connection between Mercury's mutual reception to Neptune, linking the Twelfth House with the Tenth House as a blend of intellect and imagination. If we look at the sign Leo, however, as being part of the Destruction cycle, and the Twelfth House as analogous to Pisces (the culmination of the Redemption cycle), then we can understand Hemingway's preoccupation with man cosmically trying to redeem the destructive nature of his aggrandized ego (Leo). Through this sign, he reacts to the competitiveness he feels in those close to him. But, through the House he experiences the *cosmic* ways in which he must act above the reactions of his lower self. Thus, Hemingway could inwardly feel the power of Leo, but also know (Mercury in the Twelfth House) that power is only power when it is unused. Leo is the sign of creativity. It shows the highest possible output that an individual can achieve through his lower self. Since it appears in the Twelfth House in Hemingway's chart, it indicates that this kind of output would have been the true creative expression of the author's full and complete *cosmic* being.

When we study the *decanate* placements of the planets, we find Mars to be the most outstanding planet. This would reflect the author's individualistic nature, and powerful masculine ego. At times, he was an isolationist, autonomously self-assertive, and aggressively eager to experience the primitive Mars-like qualities of life. He was concerned with man as a leader of himself, and the actual Mars placement in Virgo in his First House would reaffirm this as a rather personal crusade.

The *duads* show us another fascinating area in the chart. All of the planets in the upper hemisphere (*cosmic* quadrant) are in duads that have to do with "mind." Pluto is in the Sagittarius duad of Gemini, symbolizing the higher mind and an unconscious attunement to nature. Neptune is in the Aries duad of Gemini, indicating the personal mind fighting for itself amidst duality. Venus is in the Sagittarius duad of Cancer showing the expansiveness of emotion that was a part of Hemingway's greatness. The Sun is in the Gemini duad of Cancer, showing the need to communicate and write about one's feelings and perceptions. Finally, Mercury (the planet of writing) is in the Gemini duad of Leo, where rulership between the planet and the duad allows the best energies of the planet to creatively express themselves through the sign.

The higher *cosmic* self then, in this horoscope is very powerfully "mind" oriented. But, the lower *personal* self (through the first quadrant) finds Mars in the Taurus duad of Virgo and Jupiter in the Scorpio duad of Scorpio. Thus, there is a strong accent on physicality and the fulfillment of appetites of the lower self.

Hemingway knew how to live life to its fullest. Robust, vivid, and sometimes even childlike, he understood the changing seasons in nature and man's changing nature as part of a greater cosmic whole. With 5 mutable planets, he could adapt to the ever-changing river of ideas that flowed through him. Still, with a Fixed Ascendant (Leo) he could maintain his steady sense of identity and purpose. This combination of mutability along with fixed signs at the angles enables an individual to perceive their relationship with the world and themself as something in which everything changes—but nothing truly changes!

Change represents growth. But, change without being fixed in one's foundations is much like uprooting a tree from its original source of growth. The ability to stay fixed enough to perceive change while one is changing is the way in which a person truly evolves. With Scorpio at the nadir of the chart, Hemingway would have experienced many powerful emotional transformations at the very core of his soul. Still, amidst these transformations, the fixed quality of this sign would have sustained him through a natural awareness of inner stability.

Conclusion

*A*ll that we have talked about has been in the form of preliminaries; those very important foundations for horoscope interpretation that too many students of astrology tend to overlook. So great is the interest in signs, planetary aspects, transits, progressions and the like that a unified method of interpretation has heretofore never really been developed. These other factors (and many more) are extremely important, but they do come later. One builds a house from the ground up rather than the other way around.

To this day, only 10% of the world recognizes the great truths that can be found through this miraculous science. The unfortunate reason for this is that different schools have different ways of studying astrology and understanding what it means. With so many different frames of reference, it becomes difficult for a world looking for understanding to truly know where to begin. Thus, one either believes in astrology or doesn't. Belief, however, is not what astrology is about. *It is a system which explains natural law.* In order to see this, one must first confront the undeniable laws of the universe, the observable ways of nature, and all that man already understands as fact. Then

from what is, it becomes possible to see the connection
between the system of astrology and the order to the world.
When students and astrologers learn to do this, astrology
will no longer be a "belief", but instead be raised to the
dignity of the science that it is.

Very little emphasis was put on each individual zodiac
sign in this book for the specific reason that what we have
done was to build a solid foundation so that Sun sign
astrology never becomes the core of our understanding, but
rather an integrated part of the system of astrology as a
whole. We have hinted at the Sun signs, and alluded to
them in order to see other things. We have looked at the
Sun signs as part of the ways in which nature expresses
herself, and we have seen the different qualities inherent in
them. As we continue our study of astrology in the next
volume we will study the Sun signs in the full detail that
they deserve, seeing how they correlate with all of the
information we have learned so far. From there we will
build further our structure of astrology always keeping in
mind that it is both a fine art and a specific science.

The stronger we build this structure, the better it will
work for us; and what perhaps is even more important, the
better astrology will realize its own uniformity in a world
that so badly needs all it has to give.

There is a story of a young man who studied under a
Guru and asked his teacher, "Master what shall I study?"

The Master answered him "Study yourself, and come
back when you understand."

The student went away for forty years. Then he
returned and said "Master, I have studied myself for forty
years. What shall I do next?"

The Guru looked at him and smiled. "That is very well
Now that you have spent forty years studying yourself, go
back and do it again!"

As incredulous as this sounds, it is the way of astrology;
for astrology is a study of the self. If one can know oneself
through astrology then one can know the universe. The

important thing to realize is that in order to know astrology well, much time, care and patience is necessary. It is unquestionably a lifetime study; if not more. The student who believes that the framework of reference through which astrology views life can be understood in just a few short weeks, months or even years, is lying to himself. Twelve years ago, I knew astrology well. Seven years ago, I was not quite that sure. Today, I realize that I am just beginning to understand such a small portion of what it is all about, that each day never fails to amaze me with all there is to learn. Astrology is this way. Therefore, let us build our foundations strong before allowing ourselves to be sidetracked by all of the tangential information (which is unquestionably important) but which can so easily lead us to believe that we know what we do not know.

Ultimately it is consistency that makes one a fine astrologer and astrology itself, respectable. As we go further into exploring all that astrology can teach us we should always keep in mind that this is our goal; that consistency is the foundation of proof, and that proveability is the building blocks of confidence which ultimately allows us to use this great art and science not only for our growth, but also for the benefit of mankind.